A Very Merry
HANDPAINTED CHRISTMAS

CAROL MAYS

NORTH LIGHT BOOKS

CINCINNATI, OHIO
www.artistsnetwork.com

About the Author

Carol Mays is a decorative painter, designer, teacher and business woman. She is the author of nine books on decorative painting; this is her second North Light book. Carol has also created numerous pattern packets on both decorative and glass painting. You will find her at most of the decorative painting conventions around the country demonstrating her techniques and ideas. She and her husband, David, run their own business called A Couple of Ideas in Tulsa, Oklahoma. Carol's Web site is www.AcoupleofIdeas.com. Her previous book for North Light is called *Decorative Painting on Glass, Tile & China*.

Published by North Light Books, an imprint of F&W Publications, Inc., 4700 E. Galbraith Road, Cincinnati, Ohio 45236. (800) 289-0963. First edition.

Other fine North Light Books are available from your local bookstore or art supply store, or direct from the publisher.

07 06 05 04   5 4 3 2

Library of Congress Cataloging-in-Publication Data

Mays, Carol.
    A very merry handpainted Christmas / by Carol Mays.
        p. cm.
    Includes index.
    ISBN 1-58180-364-8 (pbk. : alk. paper)
        1. Glass painting and staining. 2. Christmas decorations.
        I. Title

TT298.M383 2003
748.5'028'2—dc21
                                                    2002044458

Editor: Gina Rath
Production Coordinator: Kristen Heller
Designer: Joanna Detz
Layout Artist: Kathy Gardner
Photographers: Tim Grondin, Christine Polomsky & Al Parrish

metric conversion chart

TO CONVERT	TO	MULTIPLY BY
Inches	Centimeters	2.54
Centimeters	Inches	0.4
Feet	Centimeters	30.5
Centimeters	Feet	0.03
Yards	Meters	0.9
Meters	Yards	1.1
Sq. Inches	Sq. Centimeters	6.45
Sq. Centimeters	Sq. Inches	0.16
Sq. Feet	Sq. Meters	0.09
Sq. Meters	Sq. Feet	10.8
Sq. Yards	Sq. Meters	0.8
Sq. Meters	Sq. Yards	1.2
Pounds	Kilograms	0.45
Kilograms	Pounds	2.2
Ounces	Grams	28.4
Grams	Ounces	0.04

Dedication

This book is dedicated to the memory of my wonderful mother, Lenora Oakley. She was my personal cheerleader, she inspired me to be creative and encouraged me to follow my dreams. Her sweet spirit is always with me.

My mother knew the secret ingredient for a magical Christmas. This secret, unselfish love, she exemplified every day of her life; but her love overflowed throughout the Christmas season. Because of this, I treasure Christmas memories, and I have learned how powerful unselfish love can be when shared with others.

Acknowledgments

I have many people to thank for making this book possible. First, thanks to John Mulvey, Diane Bower and Sue Perricone. They gave me my first opportunities with Binney & Smith, making it possible for me to grow in confidence and experience.

I also want to thank Kathy Kipp at North Light Books, for believing in me and making my relationship with North Light an enjoyable experience. Also to my photographer and new friend at North Light, Tim Grondin, for his wonderful photography and good nature which made the photo shoot such a delight.

And special thanks go to my amazing editor, Gina Rath, whose expertise I admire and whose friendship I cherish.

Finally, a big thank you to the love of my life, my husband and my friend, David, who is always there for me.

Table of Contents

Introduction

Christmas memories are permanent treasures in our lives. Each year we relive past Christmas traditions as well as generate new memories for the years to come.

It is an incredible pleasure for me to be able to present this Christmas book to you. Christmas is such an important event for me and being able to paint for my family and friends makes it even more rewarding.

Many years ago, I made all my Christmas gifts for my family and friends because there was very little extra money to spend. Now I make Christmas gifts for my special friends and family because I love and cherish their friendship, and want to share my art with those that I hold so dear. I hope this book will inspire you to create special memories for yourself and those you love.

If you have never purchased my books or patterns or have never painted with me, you will want to read the chapters on Materials and Techniques before attempting to paint the projects in this book. Painting on glass and other hard, slick surfaces requires acrylic enamel paint for guaranteeing permanency, and soft, supple brushes to guarantee success. I have described in detail the specifics of the paints and brushes I use, plus other information that will help make glass painting enjoyable for you as well as successful.

Painting on glass ornaments and tableware is easy and fun and should be attempted with that frame of mind. It is not meant to be fretted over and meticulously performed. Because of the hard, slick nature of glass, the application of paint will appear imperfect. I implore you to ignore imperfection and proceed with your painting; you will be very satisfied with the overall effect.

My hope is that you will take my designs and make them your own by embellishing them and changing them as you desire. There is an abundance of plain glassware in craft shops, discount stores and department stores just waiting for your wonderful embellishments. During the holidays you can find brightly colored glass ornaments in all sizes and shapes. If you cannot find the exact surface I have used for my projects, it is easy to find a similar piece that works just as well.

Most importantly, paint with a happy attitude and a light heart and everything else will fall into place.

CHAPTER ONE

Materials

PAINT

Acrylic Enamels for Glass

Many different brands of glass paint are on the market. Each brand has its own specific instructions that are required to ensure the durability of the paint when applied to glass and other slick surfaces. Most brands need to be baked in the home oven; baking time and temperature vary among brands, so be diligent about following the specific directions for each brand. Other brands of glass paint need special applications of conditioners and topcoats and some have specific curing times before the glassware can be used. It is imperative that you refer to the instructions before starting any project. This will ensure the durability and permanency of the finished painted glassware.

For the glass tableware and ornaments in this book, I used Liquitex Glossies acrylic enamels, made by ColArt.

Other Acrylic Paints

For the non-glass projects in this book, I used FolkArt acrylic paints made by Plaid. The paint and color information is shown at the beginning of each project.

BRUSHES

Many people become frustrated when they try to paint on glass because of the streaky and uneven coverage which results in a messy look. This is easily remedied by using the correct brush.

After years of personally experimenting with many different brands of paint and brushes, I can assure you that the streaky and messy appearance is not the fault of the paint brand. It is more likely caused by the type of brush being used.

It is imperative that you use the right kind of brushes when painting on glass. The biggest mistake most first-time glass painters make is using the same kind of synthetic brushes they use for their other acrylic painting.

Painting on glass is different than painting on other surfaces such as wood or metal. The hard slick surface of the glass will reject the springiness of synthetic brush bristles and will cause irregular paint coverage, which can be disappointing and unacceptable.

I have found that extremely soft brushes (some of which are totally useless when painting other surfaces) will provide excellent results on glass. Soft-bristled brushes will lay the paint onto the glass and will not push or spring away from the slick surface, resulting in smooth, complete coverage.

If you purchased my previous book on glass, tile and china painting, you may notice that I am using some different brushes in this book. Although I still love every brush that I used in the last book, I am continually experimenting; therefore, I have discovered some new brushes that work beautifully for the projects in this book.

These brushes are inexpensive and easy to find and they have been wonderful to use for these projects. If you own the brushes that I recommended previously, you do not need to purchase any additional brushes. They will work fine for these projects.

GLASS PAINTING BRUSHES

Royal Soft-Grip Brushes are fairly new and I have had excellent results with them. If you can't find them in your local craft store, check the Resources section in the back of this book for the manufacturer's address.

I need to explain the specifics of these Royal Soft-Grip brushes. The sizes of the flat shaders do not conform to the sizes of regular acrylic brushes. Therefore, a size 1 Soft-Grip shader would be the same size as a no. 4 flat shader in a regular acrylic brush. A size 4 Soft-Grip Shader is about the same size as a no. 8 flat shader. If you are using brushes other than the Soft-Grip, you will need to be aware of these size differences in the project instructions.

On page 10, I have listed for you my favorite brushes that make glass painting easier and more fun for me, starting with the Royal Soft-Grip brand.

• Royal Soft-Grip Series SG589 Gold Taklon script liner size 5/0. This is a nice brush for linework on glass.
• Soft-Grip Series SG595 Gold Taklon short liner size 5/0.
• Soft-Grip Series SG1250 Pure Sable round size 3.
• Soft-Grip Series SG4000 White Nylon round size 2.
• Soft-Grip Series SG4010 White Nylon shader sizes 1, 2 and 4.
• Soft-Grip Series SG4090 White Nylon flat sizes 2 and 4 (the flat has longer bristles than the shader).

The Royal Langnickel sable brush is one of my most important brushes. No other company makes a similar brush as far as I know. This is a stubby but soft brush that is useful for many glass-painting techniques. I use it for almost all drybrushing and also for dabbing in highlights and shadows when I am painting in the reverse technique.

• Royal Langnickel Series 5005 sable sizes 8, 12, 14 and 20.
• Royal Comb Series RG730 1/4 inch (6mm), used on Santa's beard in project 3.

The following brushes are used for the other, non-glass surfaces in the book. They are wonderful synthetic brushes that work well on all surfaces except glass.

• Series 2150 Royal Aqualon flat sizes 2, 6, 10 and 1/2-inch (12mm)
• Series 2170 Royal Aqualon no. 4 filbert
• Series 2250 Royal Aqualon no. 4 round
• Series 2700 Royal Aqualon 1/2-inch (12mm) flat

Optional brushes to consider are cheap (inexpensive) natural hair or sable brushes. Do not buy the expensive sable brushes as they have too much spring and the acrylic enamel paint is just too hard on them. It is not necessary to have such fine brushes for glass painting.

Another of my favorite brushes is an inexpensive sable lipstick brush. You can use this brush in place of the no. 4 flat shader that I list in many of my projects.

Experiment with various natural hair brushes and find the ones most suitable for you. With the right brush you should see an amazing difference in control and coverage.

MISCELLANEOUS SUPPLIES

• **Q-tips** These are great for cleaning up boo-boos. Just remove about half of the cotton from the end of the tip, then roll it in your fingers to tighten the remaining cotton to the stick. Dip the tightened tip in a tad of rubbing alcohol and carefully remove the mistake. Off-brand swabs do not work as well for me. I also use Q-tips to paint dots and small flower petals.
• **Wax-free transfer paper** Sally's by Saral is the brand I prefer for transferring patterns onto glass surfaces.

• **Miracle Sponge** You can cut the dry, flat Miracle Sponge into any shape, place it in water and watch it expand! Then the shape can be used to sponge paint onto the glassware.
• **Round Artist's Sponge** These are inexpensive and used to sponge paint onto glassware and ceramics.
• **Rubbing alcohol** I use rubbing alcohol for cleaning up mistakes and for cleaning the glass before painting.
• **Lint-free paper towels** I prefer Job Squad or Viva. Cheap paper towels work fine for other painting, but when painting on glass, I need soft towels that leave no lint.
• **Scotch Magic Tape** I use this for taping the pattern or design onto the glass.
• **Permanent pen** I use a permanent ink pen (such as Sakura Identi-pen) with a tiny point for tracing the pattern onto the reverse side of a glass surface.
• **Toothpicks** Toothpicks are great for making tiny dots. You can also outline with a little thinned paint on the end of a toothpick. I lightly sand the sharp tip off with an emery board so it is still pointed but dulled a bit. I also make great looking tiny flowers by making a dot and then slightly pulling to form a petal.
• **Foam Brush** for base coating large areas quickly.
• **Gloss Medium & Varnish** used for the Glitter Ornaments.
• **Leafing Adhesive Pen** also used for the Glitter Ornaments.
• **Fabric Medium** This medium can be mixed with your paints to make them permanent on fabric. I like to dampen the fabric in the design area with the fabric medium and then scrub the paint into the fabric. Do one small area at a time so the fabric medium will not dry out as you work.

GLASSWARE PREPARATION

No brand of paint will be permanent even when baked in the oven if you do not properly prepare the glassware ahead of time. This is critical to successfully painting on glassware and must be faithfully performed. The majority of failures result because of poor or no preparation.

Wash the glassware in warm sudsy water to remove all traces of oil and dirt. Rinse thoroughly and allow to dry. To remove any soap residue use lintless paper towels and wipe the surface with rubbing alcohol or a 1:1 vinegar-and-water mixture. While painting the glassware, do not touch the area to be painted with your fingers. Even if they are scrupulously clean, your hands contain oils, which will form a barrier between the paint and the glass. This will affect adhesion. Handle the glassware very carefully and try to touch it only in the places where no paint will be applied.

BAKING IN A HOME OVEN

Some people may balk at the idea of baking painted glassware in a home oven. However, this makes Liquitex Glossies and certain other brands of glass paint more permanent. I personally do not find it troublesome to bake painted glass items in my oven.

I have found that the items can either be placed on a baking sheet or directly on the oven rack with no apparent danger. I have baked all thicknesses of glass to experiment with the safety of the baking process, and I have never had a piece of glass break in the oven. Even the most fragile glass makes it through the baking process very successfully.

The items should be placed in a cool oven so the glass is allowed to heat gradually until it reaches the desired temperature. A slight odor is emitted from the oven during the baking process, but it is not annoying to me. The odor is not toxic, but if it is offensive to you, I suggest wearing a breathing mask or pick that time to do some gardening or sunbathing. As my dear husband will attest, I have had a lot worse odors coming from my oven!

BAKING A STACK OF PLATES

Because I often have entire sets of glass dishes to bake, I have discovered this time-saving technique. When I am baking a set of plates, I arrange copper pennies in stacks of four and place three or four stacks equally distributed on one plate. I then place another plate on top of these stacks of pennies, then stack more pennies, then add another plate and so on. I usually bake about eight plates per stack. Bowls can be stacked in a similar manner.

When stacking glassware in this manner, I extend the baking time by five minutes. I have never broken any dishes using this method, and the pennies do not get too hot to cause any problems. Always turn off the oven and let the dishes cool before taking them out of the oven to prevent getting burned.

USING A DISHWASHER

Many brands of paint boast that they are dishwasher safe when the proper procedures are used in the paint application process, and my own experience has confirmed this claim. However, I personally consider all of my painted glassware as highly treasured as fine china, so I recommend hand washing only.

Because of today's high-powered dishwashers and dishwashing products that contain abrasives and bleach, I do not want to gamble on even the slightest color change or fading of my painted items. On all of my pieces that I sell, I attach a fancy tag stating that they should be treated just like fine china and should be hand washed only.

SAFE TO USE?

Even though most of the glass paints on the market are non-toxic, it is not recommended that you paint on the surfaces that will come in contact with food. This puzzled me as I knew it was safe to ingest the paint itself, so why not eat from a painted plate? The reason is, when cutting food on a plate, there is a chance that the paint could be pierced with a sharp edge and cause an indentation. Even though this indentation may not be visible to the human eye, it could form a trap for bacteria to hide (similar to a crack in a plate) and thus the danger. This is the reason the paint manufacturers must say that paint should not be used on surfaces that will come in contact with food.

This brings up a special challenge when designing painted glassware that will be in contact with food. Clear glass plates can have a design in the center since they can be painted in reverse; the design is seen on the surface but the painting is actually on the underside. (See Project 6, page 55 for reverse painting.) China plates, however, should be painted on the rim only.

TRANSFERRING THE PATTERN

I have had very good luck simply tracing my pattern on using wax-free Sally's Graphite Transfer Paper by Saral. I use the gray on clear glass and the white or yellow Saral on colored glass.

Tape the pattern face down to the opposite side of the glass so it shows through to the side you are painting on.

Another option is to tape the pattern face down onto the side that you will be painting on so that it shows through to the other side. Then trace the major outlines of the pattern with a permanent pen. These lines will not be on the side that you are painting on but will actually show through from the other side.

The advantage of this is that it is a little easier to paint from the outlines than from a paper pattern. When all the painting is complete, use rubbing alcohol on a Q-tip or lint-free paper towel to remove the inked lines from the glass.

HELPFUL TIPS

• Glass paint dries fast on the palette but slow on glass. It always looks shiny so it is hard to tell by looking if it is dry or not. The paint is dry when it is no longer tacky to the touch. Remember: have patience!
• You cannot use a wet palette with this paint as it changes the consistency of the paint.
• Make sure you wipe all of the water out of your brush on a paper towel before you reload with paint.
• When you load your brush, push hard and fill the brush full of paint.
• Most of all, relax and have fun!

CHAPTER TWO

Techniques

BRUSH LOADING TECHNIQUES

Loading the brush with paint means more than sticking the brush into paint and then applying the paint to the surface. You must have a proper brush load with enough paint worked into the brush to carry it nicely over the surface without leaving ridges. Ridges result when the outside surface of the brush contains too much paint that has not been worked into the hairs.

Dip the bristles of the brush into a puddle of paint. Apply pressure as you stroke through the side of the paint. Keep stroking and applying pressure on the palette (pushing down on the hairs as shown) so you can force the paint into the bristles and not just let it remain on the outside of the bristles. When I say fully loaded it does not mean that the brush will be oozing with paint, it just means that the bristles have been filled with paint all the way through (but not all the way up to the metal ferrule) then blended so there are no heavy globs of paint on the outside edges.

This seems so simple, but without proper brush loading, it is very hard to achieve beautiful brushstrokes and nice smooth basecoating.

Loading the Brush Apply enough pressure on your brush that the paint is forced into all the bristles, not just along the outside edges.

Double Loading the Brush First, properly load your brush in the basecoat color as instructed above. Then tip one corner into the highlight color and blend the two colors together on the palette, stroking in the very same area. Sometimes I ever-so-lightly creep my brush bristles from side to side to help the colors blend together without a line.

Triple Loading the Brush Properly load the brush in the medium color, then tip one corner into the light color and the other corner into the dark color. Blend as you did for the double-loaded brush.

PAINTING TECHNIQUES

Liquitex Glossies glass paint may be mixed with water without compromising the binder or losing adhesion. A ratio of 20% water to 80% paint is safe. It is the only paint brand I know that can be floated using water. Other brands of paint provide a thinning medium to be used for floating color and for linework. If you are using another brand of paint, you must use the thinning medium for that particular brand. Do not mix brands of paint and medium as it may adversely affect the results.

Floating

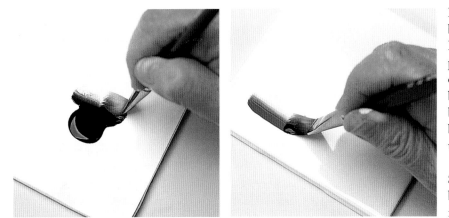

Loading a Float (Far Left) Dip the brush into the water or medium. Press the side of the brush into the paint and blend on your palette to distribute the paint. The paint should be dark on one edge and fade away before it gets to the other side of the brush. (Remember to press the brush to push the paint into the bristles.)

Straight Float (Left) Once you have the brush properly loaded you are ready to float the color. This is how it will look.

Shape-Following Strokes

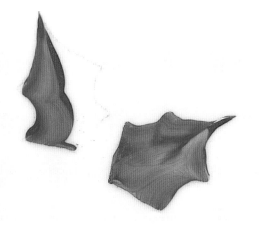

You will use shape-following strokes quite often throughout the book. This simply means to follow the shape of whatever you are painting. Choose a properly sized brush so you can cover the area with as few strokes as possible.

Tornado Stroke

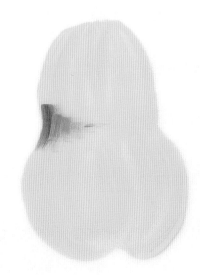

You will use the "tornado" stroke on the pear in project 2, page 29. The tornado stroke is a filler stroke that connects the top curved section to the bottom curved section.

Load the brush in a float. Starting big, walk the brush across, making each stroke smaller and smaller. This is how the finished stroke looks.

Smiley Stroke

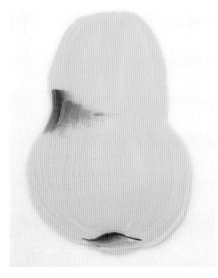

This stroke is used on the pear at the blossom end. Use a flat brush loaded for a float. Apply this stroke with just a slide, press and slide.

Lifeline with Take-a-Breath Dots

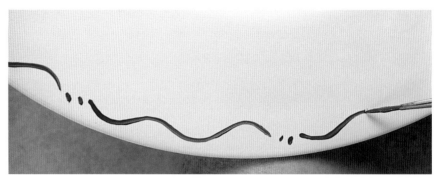

Use a script liner to paint a "lifeline," which is simply a wavy line along a border or rim. When the brush starts running out of paint, stop and make two dots (I call this "taking a breath"), reload your brush and begin the lifeline again.

Walking the Color

1

2

Use this technique when you want to float color over a wide area and one stroke isn't sufficient. Practice this technique by basecoating a strawberry shape with Orange, allow to dry. Load a flat brush with Red as a float and stroke quickly down one side of the shape.

By just lifting the brush (don't reload) and floating again right next to the first stroke, you will "walk the stroke." Keep repeating this until there is no paint left on the brush; the floated color will just disappear into the base color.

Comma Stroke

1

Use a round brush to create a comma stroke. Load the brush with paint, touch the brush then push down. The comma stroke is just one smooth stroke.

2

Lift and slide to a point to finish the stroke.

Tiny Pine Tree

1

Determine the size pine tree you want to paint, then choose the largest flat brush that is appropriate. Double load the flat brush with Pine Green and White. Hold the brush vertically and touch in the treetop.

2

Turn the brush horizontally and use light back and forth touches, making the tree wider at the bottom.

3

When the tree is the size that you want it to be, stop.

4

Side load White onto the brush and add snow to the tree by tapping the snow onto one side only.

Ribbon Stroke

The ribbon will be the width of the brush you choose. Load a flat brush and begin on the chisel edge; press, slide and lift back up. When you lift up on the brush, the ribbon will be thinner and when you press down on the brush, the ribbon will be wider. The ribbon will appear to twist and turn. Practice this stroke with different size brushes—you'll become an expert before you know it!

Graphite Paper and Tracing

1

Graphite paper can be kind of messy. I have found it helpful before using it, to always gently wipe the graphite side with a paper towel to remove any loose, excess graphite.

Wound

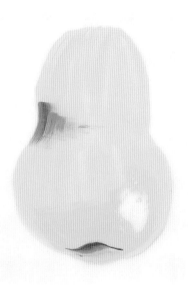

The reason you always want to make sure that the paint is thoroughly dry before adding a second coat is to prevent a "wound" such as the one shown above. If the first layer of paint is not quite dry, it will adhere to wet paint applied over it. This causes the first layer of paint to lift—leaving a wound. If this happens, you have to completely remove the paint from the surface and start over again.

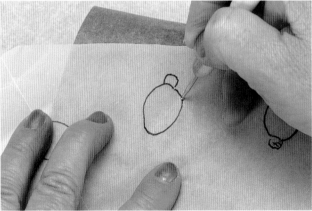

2

Place the graphite paper, graphite facing down, onto the surface. Lay the patterned tracing paper over the graphite paper, then use a stylus to trace the pattern onto the surface.

Dulling a Toothpick

To dull a toothpick, I lightly sand the sharp tip off with an emery board so it is still pointed but dulled a bit. This will be used to make dip dots or tiny flowers.

Preparing a Sponge

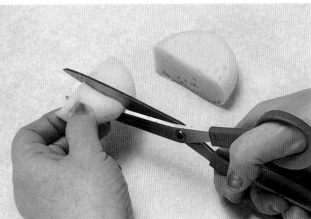

I love to use these round artist's sponges for sponging paint onto glass or other hard, reflective surfaces. They're inexpensive and give me the look I want. If you are using them for a small area, they can be cut in half or into fourths using scissors.

Helpful Tips

꙰ When using Royal Soft-Grip brushes, it is important to remember that Soft-Grip brush sizes differ from the usual decorative painting brush sizes, as described on page 8.

꙰ White bristles will get stained. It will not affect the performance of the brush.

꙰ Don't trace curlicue lines from the patterns. If you trace the lines and then try to paint them, the curlicues will look stiff and uninspired. Practice painting curlicues freehand until you feel comfortable with them.

꙰ Shading and highlighting can be done either using floated color or with double loading. When a double loaded brush will easily fit into the area to be shaded without interrupting the existing colors, then that is my preferred technique.

꙰ Floated color should be used when the area is too small to accommodate a double loaded brush. The floated color technique allows the color to be floated on without disturbing the rest of the area since the paint is loaded on one small corner and water is the vehicle that moves it along the area.

꙰ It's important to understand that your project will go through stages where it looks rather bad—but don't get discouraged. Once you add details and shading, it will all come together.

꙰ The Yellow paint in the Liquitex Glossies line is very transparent, therefore I recommend always adding a tiny touch of White when using Yellow.

꙰ When painting sets of dishes, it is easier to paint all of the same units at one time. If you are doing a set of eight plates, you would do the same step on all eight. By the time the eighth plate is finished, the first plate will be dry and ready for the next step.

Merry Christmas Plate

This is a very quick and easy project that will complement many holiday motifs and add cheer to your Christmas table. Because this project can be painted so quickly, it is a great choice for those of you who sell your work. You can paint the design on white or clear glass objects found at local craft stores, discount stores or retail department stores.

★

ROYAL BRUSHES

Series SG595 Soft-Grip Gold Taklon 5/0 short liner; Series SG4010 Soft-Grip White Nylon no. 1 short shader; Series SG4010 Soft-Grip White Nylon no. 2 short shader.

★

ADDITIONAL SUPPLIES

Rubbing alcohol, lint-free paper towels, Scotch tape, tracing paper, wax-free transfer paper, ballpoint pen or stylus.

★

SURFACE

White china plate from any craft, discount or home supply store.

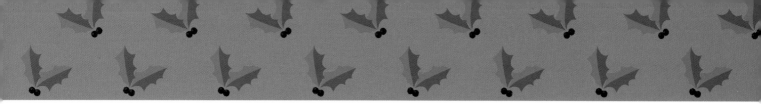

Paint and Patterns

PAINT: LIQUITEX GLOSSIES

| Red | Maroon | Green | Dark Green Mix (Maroon + Green 1:2) | White |

These patterns may be hand-traced or photocopied for personal use only. Enlarge at 154% to bring up to full size.

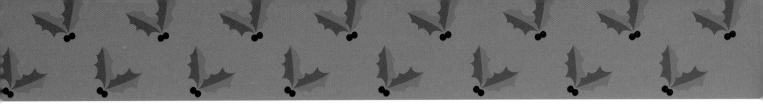

Candy Stripes

1

Clean the surface using rubbing alcohol and lint-free paper towels. Using transfer paper and tracing paper, trace on the pattern with a ballpoint pen or stylus. Just trace the outlines of the letters, not the stripes.

2

Using Maroon and your 5/0 liner, outline all the letters and the round peppermint candies.

3

Use the no. 1 shader and Red to paint in the stripes. The width of the bristles is sufficient for each stripe. Use one brushstroke for each stripe.

4

With your 5/0 liner, fill in the stripes on the round peppermint candies. Dry thoroughly. With a float of Maroon on your no. 2 shader, shade the outside edge of each Red stripe on each of the round peppermint candies.

5

With the same brush and float, also shade the inside of each candy cane letter

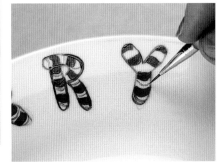

6

Use your 5/0 liner and Green to paint one thin green stripe between each Red stripe on the letters and candies.

Holly Leaves

7

Use your no. 2 shader with Green to basecoat in each holly leaf. Use shape-following strokes (see techniques, page 13).

8

To highlight the holly leaves, double load your no. 2 shader with Green and White, blend well on the palette. Paint the top edge of each holly leaf. Use shape-following strokes ending on the chisel edge of your brush.

9

Mix a dark green of Maroon and Green 1:2 and, still using your no. 2 shader, float this onto the bottom of each leaf to shade.

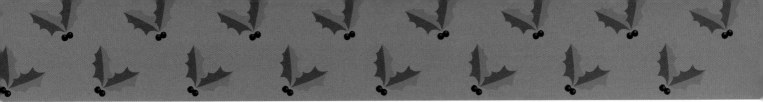

Highlights and Curlicues

10

With your 5/0 liner and White, add highlighting to each candy letter section, opposite of the side you shaded.

11

Using the same brush and paint, also highlight the peppermint candies around the outside edge of each as shown.

12

With your 5/0 liner, use the dark green mix (Maroon + Green 1:2) to pull stems into the leaves. Also add the curlicues.

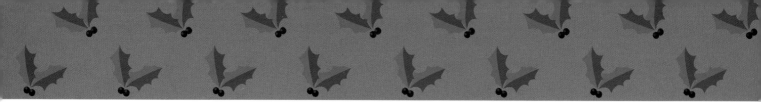

Final Touches

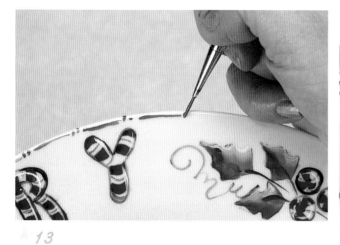

13

Thin Green slightly with water and use your 5/0 liner to add trim around the outside edge of the plate. Paint a series of short lines with two tiny dashes in between.

14

The inside trim is a wavy lifeline with two take-a breath dashes between (see page 14). Continue this around the plate as shown below.

15

Use a dulled toothpick with Maroon to add dip-dots around the holly leaves.

16

Bake your finished plate according to the paint manufacturer's instructions to make the design permanent.

Peppermint Bowl

The clear glass Peppermint Candy bowl is a very easy example of reverse glass painting. The actual painting is done on the bottom of the bowl in reverse order with the design showing through the clear glass. This bowl is an accent piece; a simple design that will complement the more elaborate plate. I chose to keep it simple by adding just a few highlights and eliminating the shading altogether.

Clean the surface with alcohol and apply the pattern to the inside bottom of the bowl. Turn the bowl over so you can see through the glass to the pattern. Begin painting the design in reverse, following the steps below.

1 Outline the candies with Maroon using the 5/0 liner brush.

2 Place highlights on the candies using White and the same liner brush as described for the plate. Let dry thoroughly.

3 Place the green accent lines on the area where the White will be painted, using the liner brush and Green. Let dry.

4 Paint the red stripes using Red and the 5/0 liner; let dry. Paint the white stripes also using the 5/0 liner. Remember the white stripes will be placed over the green lines so they will show through the front of the bowl.

5 Still using the same brush and the Dark Green mix (Maroon + Green 1:2), outline the leaves and add the center vein.

6 Double load the no. 2 shader with Green and White and fill in the leaves using shape-following strokes. Keep the white edge of the brush toward the outside of the leaf.

7 The curlicues and lines around the outside edges are made with the 5/0 liner and Green.

8 Dots are made with the sharp end of a toothpick and Maroon. Let dry thoroughly. Bake the glass bowl according to the paint manufacturer's instructions to make the design permanent.

Holiday Trivet

I HAVE ALWAYS LOVED THE TRADITIONAL DELLA ROBBIA CHRISTMAS DESIGNS OF COLORFUL FRUIT. I PAINTED THE TRIVET FOR MY SISTER, NANCY, WHO I LOOK UP TO AND LOVE VERY MUCH. THE DESIGN IS PAINTED ON A TRIVET AND A SMALL CERAMIC LOAF PAN THAT I FOUND AT A DISCOUNT STORE. IT WILL BE IDEAL FOR THOSE SPECIAL CHRISTMAS POT LUCK LUNCHEONS. YOU WILL CERTAINLY BE ABLE TO IDENTIFY YOUR DISH WHEN IT'S TIME TO LEAVE.

ROYAL BRUSHES

Series SG595 Soft-Grip Gold Taklon 5/0 short liner; Series SG1250 Soft-Grip Pure Sable no. 3 round; Series SG4010 Soft-Grip White Nylon no. 2 short shader; Series SG4010 Soft-Grip White Nylon no. 4 short shader; Series 5005 Langnickel no. 14 sable.

ADDITIONAL SUPPLIES

Rubbing alcohol, lint-free paper towels, Scotch tape, tracing paper, wax-free transfer paper, ballpoint pen or stylus.

SURFACE

Ceramic trivet from any craft, discount or home supply store.

Paint and Patterns

PAINT: LIQUITEX GLOSSIES

Orange	Yellow	Purple	Yellow Orange
Golden Brown	Brown	Red Purple	

Blue	Dark Blue Mix Red + Blue 1:2	Dark Blue Mix plus Red	Pine Green
Dark Green Mix Pine Green + Purple 8:1	White		

This pattern may be hand-traced or photocopied for personal use only. Enlarge at 173% to bring it up to full size.

This pattern may be hand-traced or photocopied for personal use only. Enlarge at 114% to bring it up to full size.

Basecoat the Fruit

1

Clean the surface with lint-free paper towels and rubbing alcohol. Trace on the pattern. Using your no. 3 round, basecoat the pear with Yellow mixed with a tiny touch of White. Using the same brush, basecoat the strawberry with Orange and the peach with Yellow Orange. Use your no. 2 shader and basecoat the grapes with Purple (the grapes will look more individualized after you highlight them). Allow the first coat to completely dry and basecoat everything a second time. This is how your trivet will look after everything is basecoated with two coats of paint.

2

Use your no. 4 shader to float Golden Brown down the left side of the pear. This is done in two sections, curve in at the top and then again on the bottom.

3

With the same brush and color, add two tornado strokes, one on each side to connect the two curved sections. Also add a little upside-down curve at the bottom of the pear. I call this my smiley face stroke (see pages 13 and 14 for the tornado and smiley face stroke techniques).

Shade and Highlight the Pear

4

Still using the no. 4 shader, add a light yellow-green tint on the right side of the pear. Use Yellow with a tiny touch of Pine Green to make a light yellow-green, then float this mixture down the right side. On the left side of the pear, float a little Orange to add a blush onto each section.

5

Use the same brush to float a couple of quick highlights of White on the right side of the pear and right above the indentation on the blossom end. If the pear still doesn't look like it connects, then take one more float-stroke down the left side of the pear using Golden Brown. Use your 5/0 liner and Brown to touch and pull little hairs from the blossom end (don't add too many); also add the stem on top. Touch in a tiny bit of White highlighting on the cut part of the stem.

Peach and Strawberry

6

With Golden Brown and Yellow Orange double loaded on your no 2. shader, add shading on the left side of the peach; also create a crevice in the center. Use the same brush with Yellow (add a tiny bit of White) and float some highlights on the far right side of the peach. Also highlight the area to the left of, and right next to, the crevice.

Float Orange down beside the Golden Brown and then walk the color (see page 14) away from the Golden Brown.

7

Float a final highlight of White over the Yellow highlights from step 6, on the outside edge of the peach and right next to the crevice. If you want the peach highlighted a little more, just touch in more White on the yellow part, just a little, not too much.

8

To paint the strawberry, side load your no. 4 shader with lots of Red, then blend on the palette to allow the paint to fade out to nothing. Float the Red down both sides, chiseling in after the first section and again on the bottom, then walk the color in toward the center.

9

Just tip the corner of your no. 4 shader into Maroon and shade the outside edges of the strawberry. This will really bring the strawberry to life if you shade just the edge (as shown); the underneath colors should still show through. Use your no. 14 sable with Yellow and White to tap in a highlight right into the center.

Grapes and Ribbon

10

Use your no. 2 shader and float a mixture of Red and Blue 1:2 around the front grapes. Highlight the front grapes using the above red and blue mixture with White 3:1. Double load this mixture with Red Purple. Since Red Purple is translucent the Purple underneath will still show through.

11

Use Red with your no. 2 shader to paint the bow. Use the chisel edge where you want the ribbon thin and press where you want the ribbon wider. Slide back up to the chisel edge where you want the ribbon thinner again (see page 16).

12

Double load the same brush with Red and White and add highlights to the top of the ribbon and to the outside of the trailing sides. To shade, float Maroon on the underneath and on the inside of the trailing sides. Add the dots using Red on a dulled toothpick; this helps to make the ribbon look neat and crisp.

13

Be sure all the paint is completely dry before adding the leaves. Use straight Pine Green and your liner brush to add the bracts on the strawberries. Mix Pine Green and Red 3:1 to make a nice dark green mixture. Double load your no. 2 shader with White and the dark green mixture and fill in the leaves using shape-following strokes. Use your liner and Pine Green to add the curlicues, outline the leaves and add the stems.

Final Touches

14

Using White and your 5/0 liner, add tiny touch-pull highlights on the bottom of each grape. Touch in tiny seeds on the strawberry with Maroon. Add tiny touches of White highlights on the strawberry bract leaf.

Trace the pear from your pattern onto a piece of tracing paper, then cut out the pear shape. Lay the paper over your trivet; you want only the pear uncovered. With an old toothbrush and Brown, run your finger down the bristles to speckle the pear. Use as little or as much as you like.

15

Bake the trivet according to the paint manufacturer's instructions. If your trivet is in a wooden frame, the wood may turn just a little darker and have a slight smell while it is baking, but it will survive just fine. The trivet will not be durable unless it is baked.

Santa Tumbler

I HAD SO MUCH FUN DESIGNING THESE STYLIZED SANTAS THAT I JUST HAD TO PUT THEM ON A VARIETY OF SURFACES. PAINT THE SANTAS ON ORNAMENTS OR ON A SET OF GLASSES AS WELL AS ANY OTHER SURFACE YOU MIGHT CHOOSE.

★

ROYAL BRUSHES

Series SG595 Soft-Grip Gold Taklon 5/0 short liner; Series RG730 Golden Taklon 1/4-inch (6mm) comb; Series SG4010 Soft-Grip White Nylon no. 2 short shader; Series SG4010 White Nylon no. 4 short shader; Series 5005 Langnickel no. 12 sable; Series 5005 Langnickel no. 20 sable.

★

ADDITIONAL SUPPLIES

Rubbing alcohol, lint-free paper towels, Scotch tape, stylus, fine-tip permanent pen, toothpick.

★

SURFACE

Clear glass tumbler from any craft, discount or home supply store.

Paint and Patterns

PAINT: LIQUITEX GLOSSIES

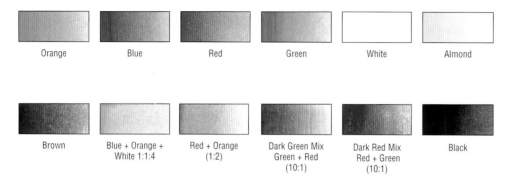

Orange	Blue	Red	Green	White	Almond

Brown	Blue + Orange + White 1:1:4	Red + Orange (1:2)	Dark Green Mix Green + Red (10:1)	Dark Red Mix Red + Green (10:1)	Black

These patterns may be hand-traced or photocopied for personal use only. They are shown here full size.

Red Stripes

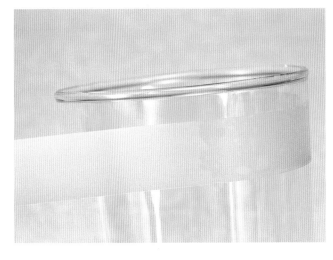

Clean the glass surface with rubbing alcohol and lint-free paper towels. Measure down at least 1-inch (25mm) from the top of the glass and mark around the glass with a fine-tipped permanent marking pen. Wrap Scotch tape around the glass right above the marks. If the glass is flared, you may have to make adjustments to the tape. Just make sure the very bottom of the tape (the area next to the marks) is smooth and flat. Don't fret over this; if it isn't perfect it won't show; the Santa will be the focal point. Apply another strip of tape ¼-inch (6mm) below the first piece of tape.

At the bottom of the glass, apply a strip of tape even with the bottom edge of the glass. Then leave ¼-inch (6mm) spacing and apply another strip above that strip. Smooth the seams with a palette knife or your thumbnail. Your Santa design should fit in the area between the Red Stripes, so you may have to adjust the size of the Santa face.

2

Use your no. 20 sable or any large soft brush to dab on Red all the way around both taped off areas. Add two coats, letting it dry thoroughly between coats.

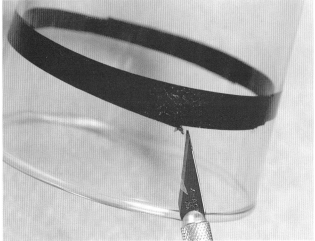

Remove the tape. If any little mistakes show after you take off the tape just use a craft knife or a single edge razor blade to clean up the area. This will not be a perfectly straight line but that's okay; it won't be noticeable once the Santa face has been added.

Santa's Beard and Face

4

Center the pattern between the red lines and tape the pattern to the inside of the glass. Use your no. 2 shader and Almond to basecoat in Santa's face; you will need two coats. Using this same brush, basecoat the beard with a light blue-gray mixture of Blue, Orange and White 1:1:4. Fill in the beard using shape-following strokes. One coat will be sufficient; you will be covering this up later with White.

A fun hint for getting the cheek colors dark enough is, "If you think they're too bright, they're just right; if you think they're just right, they're too light."

5

Load the same brush with Almond, tip the corner in Brown and shade Santa's face around the eyes, nose and mouth areas, and along both sides.

6

Load your no. 12 sable with Red and Orange 1:1 and add a tiny touch of White, then dab in the cheeks and nose. Use the 5/0 liner with the same mixture to paint Santa's mouth. The cheeks always look brighter before the rest of the detail is put on the face.

7

Use the large end of your stylus and Black to dot in Santa's eyes. When the eyes have completely dried, use the 5/0 liner and Black to add little eyelashes. Still using the same brush and Brown, darken the upper points of the mouth, also outline the bottom lip and the nose. Using the same brush, add highlights with White. Keep all the highlights on the same side, either on the right or on the left.

Santa looks a little funny without his hair and eyelashes; don't worry, this will change once we add them.

8

Use the light blue-gray mixture from step 4 with your 5/0 liner to dab in the eyebrows. Thin White with a little bit of water. Load the ¼-inch (6mm) comb by pushing down hard into the White so the brush hairs are well separated and completely filled with paint. Paint the beard using shape-following strokes; also paint the mustache. This will take approximately three coats of paint; make sure each coat is completely dry before adding the next coat. If the beard seems to need more coverage on the ends, you can stroke up from the ends and in toward the face.

9

Still using the same brush and paint, add little soft hairs around the face; also tap White into the eyebrows.

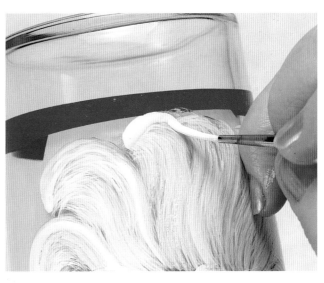

10

Use your 5/0 liner and White to define the beard further by outlining each separate beard section. Work from the ends in toward the face.

Hat and Final Touches

Using your no. 4 shader, basecoat Santa's hat with Red. Once this has dried, add a second coat of Red. Make a darker red mixture of Red and Green 10:1 and use your no. 4 shader to tap in shading around the brim and near the tassel end of the hat. Double load the same brush with White and Red and add a highlight along the top edge of the hat.

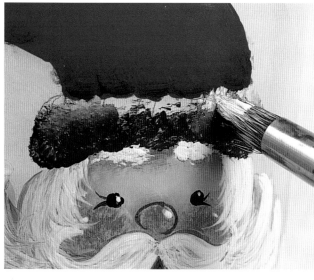

12

For the hat brim, make a dark green mixture of Green and Red 10:1 and use your no. 12 sable to pounce the mixture in along the bottom. Side load with White and tap in the top section of the brim as shown; also tap in the tassel (see step 13 at right).

13

Once this has completely dried, use your 5/0 liner and White to add the stripes on the hat brim in sets of two. Use a dulled toothpick to add White dots on the hat and on the red stripes going around the glass. Let those dry, then remove the pattern from inside the glass.

14

Bake the Santa tumbler according to the paint manufacturer's instructions. Below are three frosted glass ornaments each with a slightly different version of the Santa faces that were painted on the tumblers. Because the ornaments are much smaller, the faces are not nearly as detailed. I outlined the edge of each ornament with Red to draw attention to their shape.

Gingerbread Kids

Y OU CAN SERVE DRY FOODS ON PAINTED ITEMS, SO TRY PAINTING THIS
WHITE CHINA PLATE TO HOLD COOKIES FOR SANTA. PUT THE REST OF
THE COOKIES INTO THE COOKIE JAR AND WATCH THEM DISAPPEAR!
BOTH THE WHITE CERAMIC COOKIE PLATE AND THE LIDDED COOKIE JAR CAN BE
FOUND AT HOME DECORATING AND DISCOUNT STORES. IF YOU CAN'T FIND A NICE
COOKIE PLATE, A CERAMIC PIE PLATE WOULD WORK JUST AS WELL.

ROYAL BRUSHES

Series SG595 Soft-Grip Gold Taklon 5/0 short liner; Series SG1250 Soft-Grip Pure Sable
no. 3 round; Series SG4010 Soft-Grip White Nylon no. 2 short shader; Series SG4010
Soft-Grip White Nylon no. 4 short shader; Series 5005 Langnickel no. 14 sable.

ADDITIONAL SUPPLIES

Rubbing alcohol, lint-free paper towels, tracing paper,
wax-free transfer paper, round artist's sponge, stylus.

Paint and Patterns

PAINT: LIQUITEX GLOSSIES

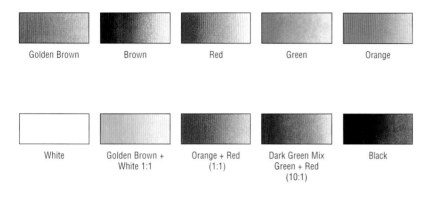

Golden Brown	Brown	Red	Green	Orange

White	Golden Brown + White 1:1	Orange + Red (1:1)	Dark Green Mix Green + Red (10:1)	Black

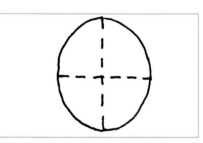

1 Divide the face into 4 sections.

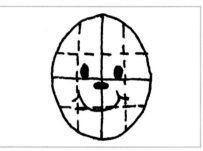

2 Divide each section again.

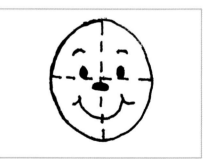

3 Place the eyes above the line and the nose below the line.

This pattern may be hand-traced or photocopied for personal use only. Enlarge at 200% to bring it up to full size.

Basecoating and Faces

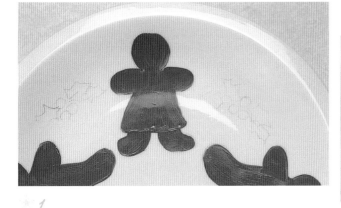

1

Clean the surface with rubbing alcohol and lint-free paper towels. Use tracing paper and transfer paper to trace the pattern onto the front of the plate (see page 16). With your no. 3 round and Golden Brown, use shape-following strokes to basecoat the gingerbread kids. You will need two coats of Golden Brown; make sure the first coat dries thoroughly before applying the next coat. If the gingerbread kids look a little ragged at this point that's okay, the highlighting will fix that.

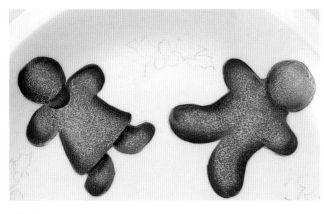

3

Use your no. 4 shader and float Brown around all of the outside edges of each gingerbread kid.

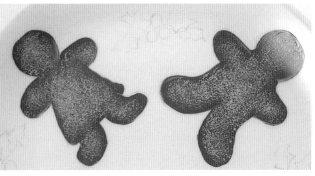

2

Mix Golden Brown and White 1:10. Cut an artist's sponge into fourths (see page 17), round the sponge into a little ball and dip it into the paint mixture. Tap on your palette to distribute the paint, then lightly sponge the mixture over the Golden Brown basecoat to create a "cookie" texture.

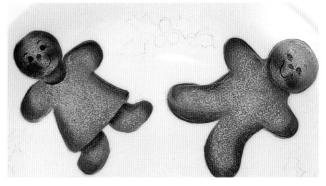

4

When the gingerbread kids are dry, replace the pattern and trace on the faces. Or you can easily draw the faces on the gingerbread kids by using the diagram instructions on page 44. Divide the face as shown on the diagram. Place the nose right under the center line where the lines meet. The eyes are placed above the center line and near the two vertical lines going down each side of the nose It is a very easy way to draw simple faces and gives you more freedom to make your own personality show up in your work.

Lightly dab in the cheeks with the Orange + Red 1:1 mix using the no. 14 sable. Use your 5/0 liner and Black to add the eyes, these are just little circles; also add the eyelashes and eyebrows, as shown. With the same brush, use Red to add little round noses and Black for their mouths.

Gingerbread Accents

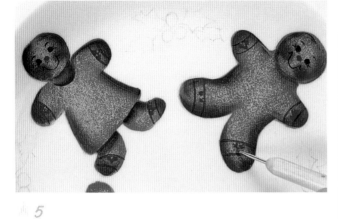

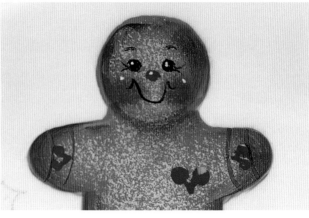

5

Still using your 5/0 liner with Green, add two little stripes on each arm and leg. Use the large end of your stylus with Red to add two dots right next to each other (don't allow the dots to touch or the paint will run together). Immediately use the small end of your stylus to pull the two dots down to a point. This will create a heart shape.

6

Make the large hearts on the front of the kids with Red and the brush handle of a large brush (your no. 4 shader should be large enough), then use the stylus to pull the heart to a point. Allow this to dry thoroughly. Using White and your 5/0 liner, add tiny dots of White on the left side of each eye, on the nose and on the outside edge of each cheek.

7

Paint the boy's hair using a 5/0 liner and White. The hair is just one large touch-and-pull stroke in the center and two smaller touch-and-pull strokes on each side. With the same brush and paint add the wavy piping around the edges. Use a pointy toothpick with White to add the dots.

8

Use your 5/0 liner and White and paint little curlicues for the girl's hair. Finish the piping and dots as you did for the boy.

Holly Leaves and Berries

9

Paint the leaves with a dark green mixture of Green and Red 10:1. Double load this mixture with White using your no. 2 shader. Keep the White facing outward and fill in the leaves using shape-following strokes (see page 13). Use your 5/0 liner to add curlicues. With Red on a no. 2 shader, basecoat the berries; allow to dry then highlight with a double-load of Red and White. Once dry, shade them with a float of Red darkened with a touch of Green.

10

Add the graduated dots around the plate rim using the handle of the 5/0 liner brush. Dip the brush handle into the paint and reload after every 5 dots, this creates the variation in size. Paint one row with Red and the other row with the dark green mixture that you used for the holly leaves (step 9). You will need to mix up a new batch of this mixture so that the paint is the right consistency.

Let the design dry overnight, then bake according to the paint manufacturer's instructions.

Cheerful Cheese Dome

I THINK THE BEST PART OF PAINTING IS SHARING OUR ART WITH THOSE WE LOVE. THIS CHEESE DOME AND ACCOMPANYING TABLEWARE WILL GRACE THE TABLE OF MY SISTER, ELIZABETH, WHO IS ALSO MY VERY SPECIAL FRIEND. SHE GRACIOUSLY AND LOVINGLY OPENS HER HOME AT CHRISTMAS FOR OUR VERY LARGE FAMILY TO GATHER AND SHE LOVES EVERY MINUTE OF IT!

TRY PAINTING THIS DESIGN ON SEVERAL ITEMS TO CREATE A MATCHING SET. YOU SHOULDN'T HAVE ANY TROUBLE FINDING THE ACCESSORIES; I FOUND ALL OF THEM AT A LARGE DISCOUNT STORE. I HAVE ALSO SEEN THEM AT MY LOCAL HOBBY CENTER.

ROYAL BRUSHES

Series SG589 Soft-Grip Gold Taklon 5/0 script liner; Series SG1250 Soft-Grip Pure Sable no. 3 round; Series SG4010 Soft-Grip White Nylon no. 2 short shader.

ADDITIONAL SUPPLIES

Rubbing alcohol, lint-free paper towels, tracing paper, Scotch tape.

SURFACE

Glass cheese dome from any craft, discount or home supply store.

Pattern and Paints

PAINT: LIQUITEX GLOSSIES

Green   Blue   Red   Pine Green   White   Gold   Yellow Orange   Maroon

Dark Green Mix Maroon + Pine Green 1:4   Green + White 1:3   Yellow Orange + White 2:1   Copper   Black + Copper 1:1   Copper + Gold 1:1   Red + White 1:1

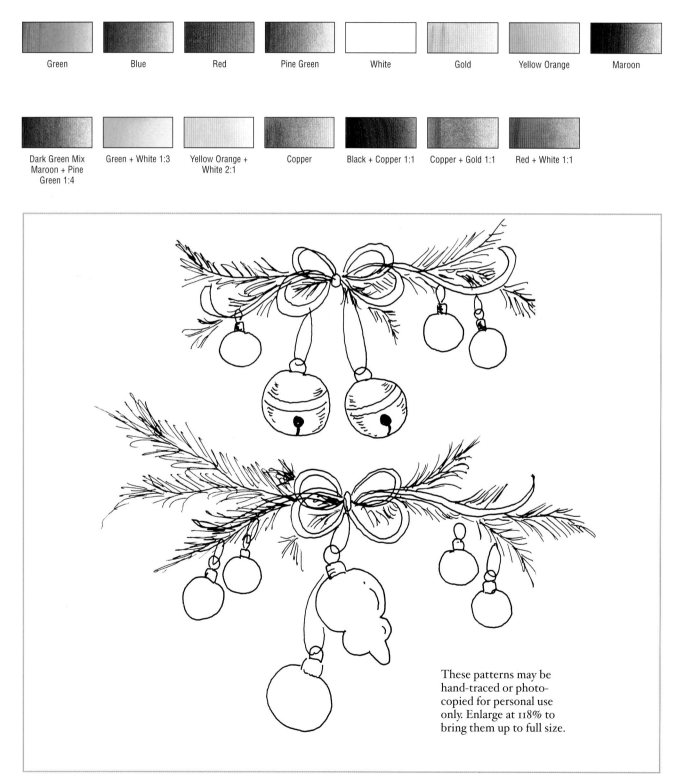

These patterns may be hand-traced or photo-copied for personal use only. Enlarge at 118% to bring them up to full size.

Pine Needles and Branches

1

Clean the glass with lint-free paper towels and rubbing alcohol. Trace the pattern onto tracing paper then tape the pattern inside the glass cheese dome. Begin by painting all of the pine branches and needles; you'll be using three different values of green for this. Add a small amount of Maroon to Pine Green 1:4; this is your darkest value of Green. Use your 5/0 script liner and paint the branches. With the same brush and paint, add needles to each branch; begin at the branch and pull out.

2

Use the same brush with Pine Green (the middle value of green) to add more needles; apply these randomly throughout the branches.

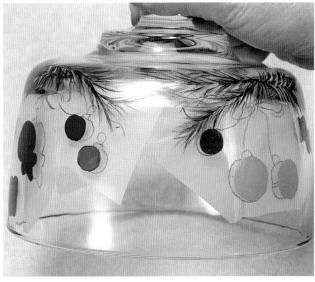

4

For some sparkle, add a few golden needles here and there using the same brush and Gold. Let dry. Basecoat the brass bells with Yellow Orange and White 2:1 using your no. 3 round. Basecoat the blue, red and green ornaments with the no. 3 round. Let everything dry, then apply a second coat to the bells and ornaments.

3

Make the lightest value of green by mixing Green and White 1:3 and with your 5/0 script, add a few needles here and there. Notice how the three values give the branches depth and dimension.

Bells and Ornaments

5

Using the no. 2 shader and Copper, float shading above and below the center band on the bells; also add a little around the top (keep this light). Still using Copper, add the little hole with your 5/0 script liner.

7

With your no. 2 shader, float Copper down both sides of each bell. Use your 5/0 script liner with White to highlight the outside edge of the shaded side of the hole. This is very subtle, but it makes a big difference. Dab in a bright highlight on the top part of each bell and in the middle of the band using your no. 2 shader with White. Also, using your 5/0 script, add a sparkle of Gold to the hangers.

If the ornament colors get too dark after you shade them, soften them up with their base color.

6

Use your no. 2 shader and float Gold around the outside edges of each bell. This color is very transparent, it really just gives the bells a shine.

Using a 5/0 script liner and a mixture of Black with Copper 1:1, darken one side of the hole. Also pull a line halfway across the top and bottom of the band on both bells. Add more lines above and below the band, making them shorter as you move away from the band. Also paint the little hangers on top.

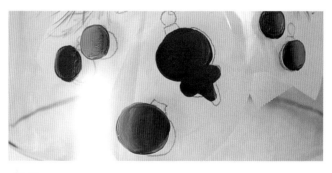

8

All the rest of the ornaments are highlighted with a double-loaded no. 2 shader. Use the basecoat color of each ornament double loaded with White (use plenty of White so they are nice and bright). Highlight whichever side you want, but only one side on each ornament.

Only the red and green ornaments are shaded. To shade the small red ornament, float Maroon onto the side of the ornament that is not highlighted. For the large red ornament, double load your brush with Maroon and Red.

To shade the green ornaments, mix a tiny bit of Red into Green to create a dark green mixture; float this onto the side opposite the highlights. The blue ornaments are not shaded.

If you need to smooth out the edges of the ornaments, use your 5/0 script liner with each ornament's base color.

Hangers and Bows

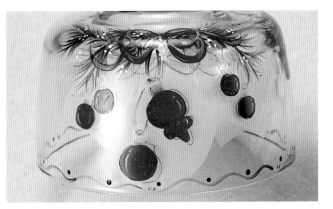

9

Use White on your 5/0 script liner and add a line of high-lights to the highlighted side of each ornament. Use Gold on the same brush to paint in the hanger tops on each ornament. Allow to dry thoroughly.

And a touch of Copper with your 5/0 script liner near the base of each hanger where it attaches to the orna-ment. Mix Copper and Gold 1:1 and add little loop wires to each hanger.

10

Mix Copper and Black 1:1 and with your 5/0 script liner, add loops to connect the ornaments to the pine branches. Paint the ribbon bows with Red. Let dry. Add highlights here and there on the bow with Red and White 1:1.

Use a dulled toothpick and wherever you like add some Gold and some White dip dots in clusters of three. With your 5/0 script liner and Pine Green, add a wavy lifeline (see page 14) around the bottom of the cheese dome. Use the brush handle end to add the green dots above the line.

11

Bake the cheese dome following the paint manufacturer's instructions.

Snowman Platter

Snowmen continue to be popular subjects to paint and I have to admit they are one of my favorites. They are also one of the easiest to paint in the "reverse painting" technique. So if you have never painted in reverse (or even if you have), grab a clear glass plate and all your supplies and let's paint!

You shouldn't have any problem finding clear glass items to paint. I found the pitcher and goblets for this project at a large discount store, and the round platter and ornament came from a craft store.

Royal Brushes

Series SG595 Soft-Grip Gold Taklon 5/0 short liner; Series SG4000 Soft-Grip White Nylon no. 2 round; Series SG4010 Soft-Grip White Nylon no. 2 short shader; Series SG4090 Soft-Grip White Nylon no. 4 flat (this brush has longer bristles than the shader and will cover large areas smoothly); Series 5005 Langnickel no. 14 sable; Series 5005 Langnickel no. 20 sable.

Additional Supplies

Rubbing alcohol, lint-free paper towels, tracing paper, fine-tip permanent marking pen, wax-free transfer paper, Scotch tape, round artist's sponge.

Surface

Clear glass platter from any craft, discount or home supply store.

Pattern and Paints

PAINT: LIQUITEX GLOSSIES

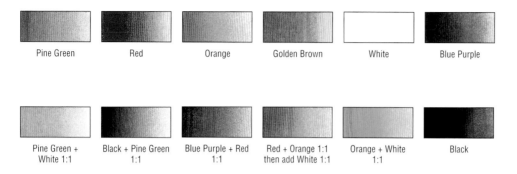

Pine Green   Red   Orange   Golden Brown   White   Blue Purple

Pine Green + White 1:1   Black + Pine Green 1:1   Blue Purple + Red 1:1   Red + Orange 1:1 then add White 1:1   Orange + White 1:1   Black

This pattern may be hand-traced or photocopied for personal use only. It is shown here full size.

This pattern may be hand-traced or photocopied for personal use only. Enlarge at 200 percent to bring up to full size.

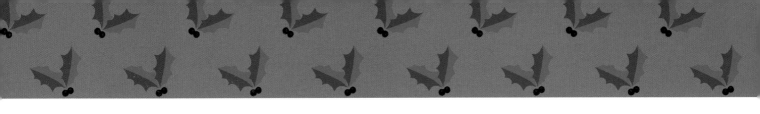

Highlights and Outlining

1

Clean the glass surface using lint-free paper towels and rubbing alcohol. This project is painted in reverse. Begin by taping the pattern onto the back of the platter. Trace the snowman pattern onto the front using a fine-tipped permanent marking pen. Remove the paper pattern. The holly on the rim of the platter is not painted until the center is painted and thoroughly dry.

2

Flip the platter over; you will now be painting on the back. In the reverse painting technique, you start with the final details of the design and work toward the beginning basecoats. Using your 5/0 liner and White, first you must place the highlighting for the nose, cheeks and eyes. Also add highlights on the holly berries and highlights for the decorative polka dots on the scarf and hat. The background has been darkened on this photo so you can clearly see where to place the highlighting.

3

Still using the 5/0 liner, follow the pattern and outline the mouth and eyebrows with Black. Thin the paint with just a little bit of water and very gently outline around the head and the scarf. Turn the platter over to check it and see how it is looking from the front. If you need to correct anything, now is the time; it will be more difficult once you paint over the highlighting and outlining.

Pine Branches and Carrot Nose

Mix Pine Green and White 1:1 and with your 5/o liner add four or five strokes to each pine branch to serve as a highlighting for the needles. Allow this to dry thoroughly before proceeding to the next step.

Use straight Pine Green to add the rest of the pine needles with your 5/o liner. Give the needles more dimension by adding a few darker needles between them with a darker mixture of Black and Pine Green 1:1. Use a 5/o liner and Black to fill in the eyeballs and add a couple of eyelashes. This photo is from the front of the platter. It's good to turn your work over often to see how it's looking from the front.

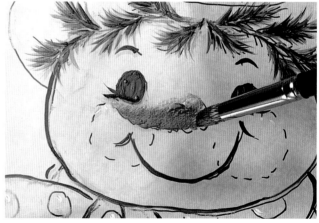

Turn the platter over to the back again and tap in the snowman's carrot nose with a double load of Orange and a little White on a no. 20 sable. Keep the White facing toward the top for a highlight.

Double load the same brush with Orange and a little Golden Brown and as you tap keep the Golden Brown to the bottom of the nose to shade it. The Orange will meet in the middle of the nose and helps create roundness to the carrot.

Cheeks and Polka Dots

8

Using your no. 20 sable with a mixture of Red and Orange 1:1 and a tiny bit of White 4:1, add the cheeks. Load the sable and really press the paint into the brush on your palette. You don't want the brush really wet, you just want the paint worked into the bristles. Remove the paint from the outside of the bristles by wiping off the excess paint onto a paper towel. The paint that comes off the brush onto the plate should be from the inside of the bristles, in a drybrush manner. (You want the cheeks to look soft around the edges.) Tap the brush lightly onto the cheek area; don't go over it too many times as it may begin to lift. Tap the cheek color right over the carrot nose.

9

Double load the no. 14 Sable with Red and White. Tap on the palette to blend the paint so the White isn't too stark. Dab polka dots onto the scarf. with just one or two dabs per dot. Also, paint in the polka dots and holly berries on the hatband using the same color and brush.

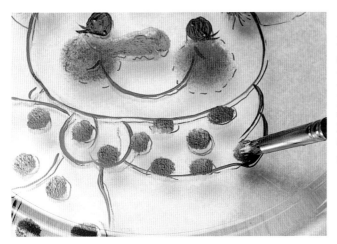

10

Clean up the edges by outlining each polka dot with Red using your 5/0 liner.

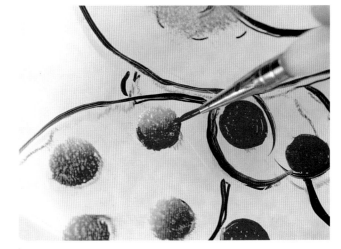

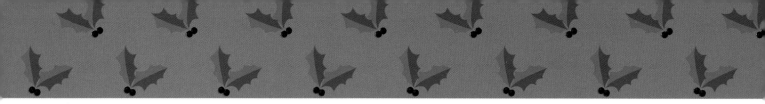

Scarf and Hatband

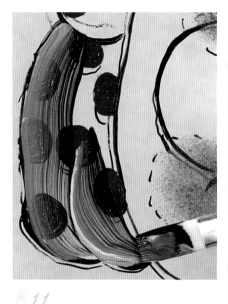

11

To paint highlights on the scarf, turn the plate 90° so it's easier to stroke. Double load a no. 4 flat with Blue Purple and White. Stroke in the longer part, keeping the White to the left. Add a shorter stroke halfway across and right next to the first stroke without touching it as shown.

12

Finish the rest of the highlighted area on the scarf and let dry. Paint holly leaves on the snowman's hatband with a double load of Pine Green and White. Then paint the hatband highlights with a double load of Blue Purple and White. Let dry completely.

13

Cover the scarf and hatband with Blue Purple. You will need two coats. Make sure the first coat is thoroughly dry before adding the second coat.

14

Turn the platter over to the front and see how the snowman looks at this point.

Remember to keep checking the front of the plate to see how your colors are looking.

Scarf, Hat, and Face

15

Double load your no. 2 round with Blue Purple and White and add the fringe using simple comma strokes. It's okay to pull the strokes up over the scarf area when you paint them, as this won't show from the front (see above). Once the fringe has dried, use black and a 5/0 liner to outline in a free-flowing manner along the outside of the fringe. Don't try to define each section.

If your paint goes outside of your outlining, you can always scrape it off with a razor blade after it has dried.

16

Double load your no. 4 flat with Black and White and outline the hat and brim, keeping the White to the outside edges. Allow this to dry completely.

17

Use the same brush and Black to fill in the hat using shape-following strokes. You will need two coats (let dry thoroughly between coats). Double load your no. 20 sable with Blue Purple and White, then barely touch into Golden Brown. Pounce around the eyes, nose and edges of the face. Every so often, add more Blue Purple or Golden Brown. Alternating these colors keeps the edges from being only one color all the time. Just make sure the darker color is always toward the outside edges, and keep the White side of the brush toward the inside. This gives roundness to the snowman's head.

Face and Holly

18

Load the no. 20 sable with White and tap in the rest of the face area. If you want a second coat of White, wait until the first coat completely dries. Turn the plate over and remove the pattern lines from the front using alcohol. Check all the colors from the front and if there are any areas in the face or hat you want covered more thoroughly, touch them up at this time.

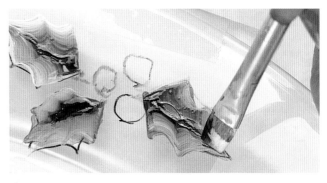

19

Wipe off the platter rim with alcohol, and try not to touch the rim where you will now be painting. Tape the holly pattern to the back of the platter rim and use a fine-tip pen to trace the pattern. You will be painting on the front of the rim. Basecoat each leaf using your no. 2 shader and Pine Green. Allow to dry thoroughly. Triple load the shader by first loading the brush with Pine Green, then tip one corner into White and the other corner into a mixture of Pine Green and Blue Purple 4:1. Stroke over the basecoated leaf, keeping the white part of the brush to the outside edge and the dark side of the brush toward the middle of the leaf.

20

With your 5/0 liner and a mixture of Blue Purple and Pine Green 4:1, outline the dark side of each leaf. Basecoat the berries using your no. 2 shader and Red. Allow this to dry thoroughly, then highlight the berries by double loading with a mixture of Orange and White 1:1 on one side of the brush and Red on the other.

21

Mix Blue Purple and Red 1:1 and with the no. 2 shader, float this mixture onto the opposite side from the highlight to shade the berries. Add curlicues with the Pine Green and Blue Purple mixture from the previous step using your 5/0 liner.

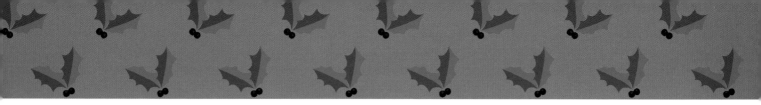

Painting the Pitcher

22

Bake the platter according to the paint manufacturer's instructions.

If you want to paint the snowman on the outside of a pitcher or goblet or on round ornaments, first adjust the size of the pattern to fit. Tape the pattern to the inside of the pitcher or goblet; it's helpful to cut slices around the edges of the pattern so you can push the pattern against the sides, as shown above.

Use the same colors you used for the platter. The pitcher and goblet are not reverse-painted; just paint the design on the outside in this order: Basecoat the hat, snowman's face and scarf. Add shading to the face; then add the cheeks and facial features. Paint the pine branches, starting with the darkest color and finishing with the highlight color. Add highlights on the hat, scarf and hatband. Add the polka dots on the scarf and hatband. Highlight the dots using the liner brush.

Poinsettia Plate

ADD A TOUCH OF ELEGANCE TO YOUR TABLE THIS HOLIDAY SEASON. THIS PROJECT PROVES THAT SOMETHING CAN BE EASY TO PAINT YET STILL LOOK REFINED AND ELEGANT.

IF YOUR CHRISTMAS DECOR DOES NOT FOLLOW THE TRADITIONAL RED AND GREEN, THE POINSETTIA COULD BE PAINTED IN ANOTHER COLOR. YOU'LL FIND IT'S EASY TO MAKE THIS DESIGN WORK AND COMBINE WELL WITH OTHER HOLIDAY MOTIFS.

ROYAL BRUSHES

Series SG4010 Soft-Grip White Nylon no. 2 short shader;
Series SG595 Soft-Grip Gold Taklon 5/0 short liner.

ADDITIONAL SUPPLIES

Rubbing alcohol, lint-free paper towels, wax-free transfer paper,
tracing paper, ballpoint pen or stylus, toothpicks.

SURFACE

White china plate from any craft, discount or home supply store.

Paint and Patterns

PAINT: LIQUITEX GLOSSIES

Pine Green Red Maroon Orange White Gold Orange + White 1:1

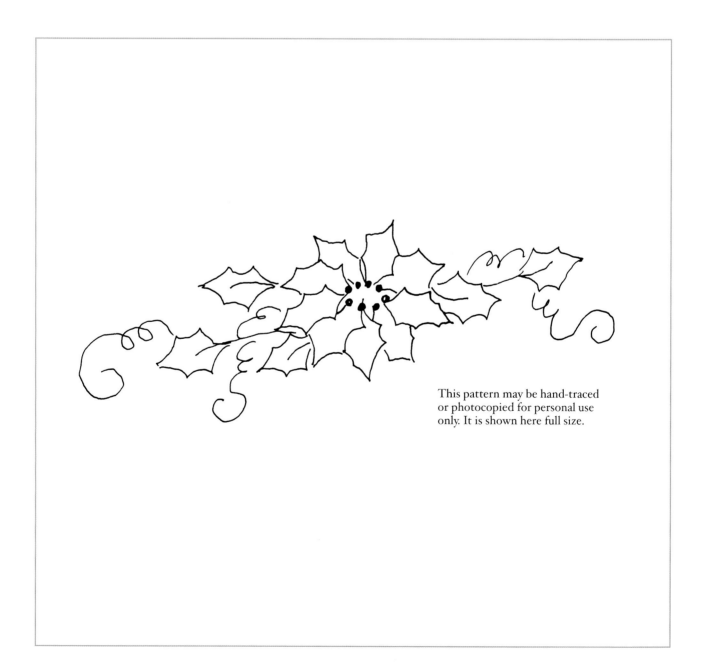

This pattern may be hand-traced or photocopied for personal use only. It is shown here full size.

Petals and Leaves

1

Clean the surface with alcohol and a lint-free paper towel. Trace on the pattern. With your no. 2 shader, basecoat the flower petals in Red, using shape-following strokes (see page 13). Float Maroon shading on the underneath petals as shown. It's okay if the petals look a little messy at this stage of the project.

2

Mix Orange and White 1:1 and use the same brush to highlight the petals. Turn the plate around so you can more easily float the highlight opposite the shaded side on each petal.

3

Using your 5/0 liner, outline every petal with Maroon thinned slightly with water. The outlining really cleans up the poinsettia. Double load your no. 2 shader with Pine Green and White and work the paint into the brush thoroughly. Keep the White toward the outside edges and use shape-following strokes to fill in the leaves.

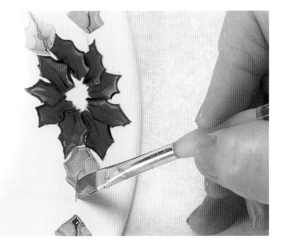

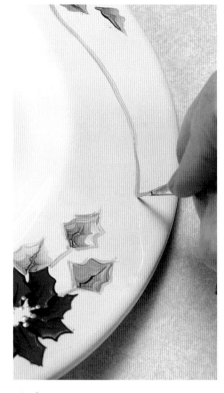

4

Using your 5/0 liner, outline the leaves with Gold. Also add the Gold line between the flower clusters.

5

Load the 5/0 liner with Pine Green and add curlicues. Use a blunt toothpick with Gold to add little gold dots randomly in the flower center, leaving some of the white of the plate showing through for the center of the poinsettia.

6

Also add Gold dip-dots in sets of three around the poinsettia.

Punch Glasses and Pitcher

7

Bake the plate according to the paint manufacturer's instructions.

If you choose to paint this design on clear glass items such as the punch glasses and pitcher shown above, you do not need to outline the leaves with Gold; the Gold is so translucent that it will not show up on clear glass.

Holiday Lights

THIS PROJECT WOULD BE PERFECT FOR A FESTIVE CHRISTMAS LUNCHEON. I HAVE ALWAYS WANTED TO HAVE A SPECIAL PARTY USING MY PAINTED TABLEWARE AND LET EACH GUEST TAKE HOME THEIR OWN PLACE SETTING. THIS MAY BE THE YEAR THAT I TRY TO DO JUST THAT.

THE CLEAR PLATES AND WINE GLASSES CAN BE FOUND AT ANY CRAFT OR DISCOUNT STORE. LOOK FOR OTHER ITEMS THAT WILL COMPLEMENT THIS EASY-TO-PAINT DESIGN, SUCH AS THE OIL-AND-VINEGAR CRUET SHOWN HERE.

ROYAL BRUSHES

Series SG595 Soft-Grip Gold Taklon 5/0 short liner; Series SG1250 Soft-Grip Pure Sable no. 3 round; Series SG4010 Soft-Grip White Nylon no. 2 short shader.

ADDITIONAL SUPPLIES

Lint-free paper towels, rubbing alcohol, tracing paper, Scotch tape.

SURFACE

Clear glass wine goblet from any craft or home supply store.

Paint and Patterns

PAINT: LIQUITEX GLOSSIES

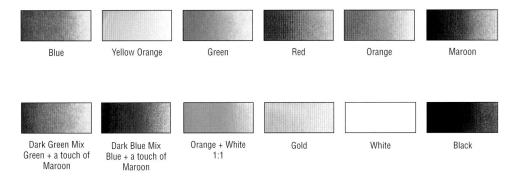

Blue   Yellow Orange   Green   Red   Orange   Maroon

Dark Green Mix
Green + a touch of
Maroon

Dark Blue Mix
Blue + a touch of
Maroon

Orange + White
1:1

Gold

White

Black

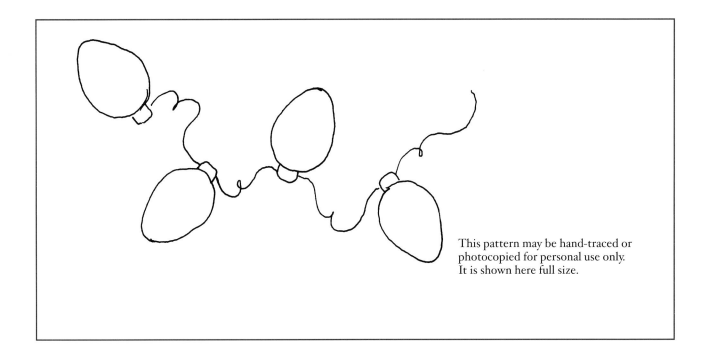

This pattern may be hand-traced or photocopied for personal use only. It is shown here full size.

Basecoating and Shading

2

Using your no. 3 round, basecoat the lightbulbs using Green, Yellow Orange, Red, and Blue. Allow the basecoat to thoroughly dry, then add a second coat.

1

Using alcohol and lint-free paper towels, clean the surface of the glass. Trace the pattern onto tracing paper. Cut the lightbulbs out individually and tape them randomly around the inside of the glass. Space them however you like, turning them in different directions. I have eight lights inside my glass; you can have more or less, whichever you like. Just make more copies if you want more lights. Your glass doesn't have to be exactly like mine; design it for your particular glass size.

3

Double load the no. 2 shader with the following colors to shade and highlight each lightbulb. Shade the green bulb by mixing Green with a touch of Maroon (just enough to darken the Green) and double loading the brush with this dark green mixture and Green. Shade down one side of the bulb. To shade the red light bulb, double load Red with Maroon and shade down one side of the bulb. The blue bulb is shaded using a touch of Maroon mixed with Blue (just enough Maroon to darken the Blue). Double load Blue and the dark blue mixture and shade down one side of the bulb. Shade the Yellow Orange bulb by double loading Yellow Orange and Orange and shading down one side of the bulb.

Highlighting

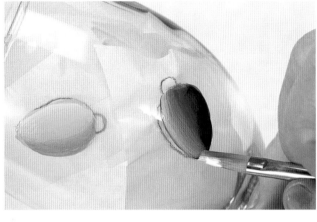

4

With the no. 2 shader, highlight the Blue, Green, and Yellow Orange lightbulbs by double loading the base color of each light bulb with White. Run the highlight down the side of the bulb opposite from the shading.

For the red light bulb, mix Orange and White 1:1; double load this light orange mixture with Red and highlight the opposite side of the light bulb from the shaded side. If the light orange color doesn't show enough, add a little more White to the mixture.

5

Use your 5/0 liner with Gold and with just two strokes, paint in the base of each light bulb.

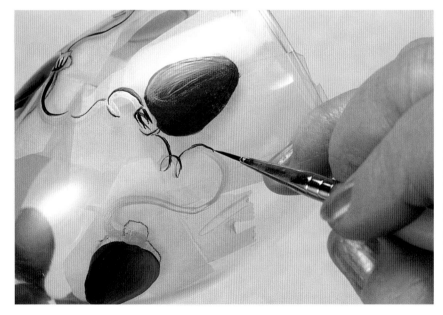

6

Load the 5/0 liner with Gold and paint the cord connecting the bulbs using curlicues. Create your own carefree pattern of ups and downs and loop-de-loops. Do not thin the Gold; it is already translucent.

With the same brush and thinned Black, outline around each base and add little lines halfway across the base. Very lightly add black outlines to the gold cord connecting the bulbs. Keep the black lines thinner than the gold lines. If you feel it is needed, you can outline the shaded side of each bulb with a thin line of Black.

Finished Goblet, Plate and Cruet

7

Bake the goblet following the paint manufacturer's instructions. The plate shown below is finished off with a Gold rim. Let the painted lightbulb design dry completely before painting the rim. Don't forget to clean the rim with alcohol before you paint.

Plaid Ribbon Set

I LOVE TO PAINT ON FABRIC AS WELL AS ON CHINA AND GLASS, AND I LOVE HOW WONDERFULLY THEY CAN COMPLEMENT EACH OTHER. ADD SOME CANDLES, LOWER THE LIGHTS AND HAVE A ROMANTIC CHRISTMAS DINNER USING THIS PAINTED ENSEMBLE.

I USED THE SAME BRUSHES FOR THE PLATE, TABLE RUNNER AND NAPKIN, BUT THE PAINT FOR EACH SURFACE IS DIFFERENT. THE COLOR CHART ON THE NEXT PAGE SHOWS WHICH PAINT TO USE FOR EACH SURFACE.

ROYAL BRUSHES

Series SG589 Soft-Grip Gold Taklon 5/0 script liner; Series SG4090 Soft-Grip White Nylon no. 2 flat; Series 2170 Royal Aqualon no. 4 filbert.

ADDITIONAL SUPPLIES

Rubbing alcohol; lint-free paper towels; tracing paper; transfer paper; deli, freezer or palette paper; fabric medium.

SURFACE

China plate from any craft, discount or home supply store. Fabric table runner and napkin (polyester/cotton) from any fabric or home supply store.

Paint and Patterns

PAINT FOR CHINA PLATE: LIQUITEX GLOSSIES

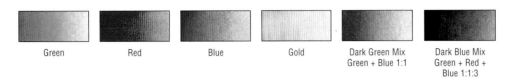

| Green | Red | Blue | Gold | Dark Green Mix Green + Blue 1:1 | Dark Blue Mix Green + Red + Blue 1:1:3 |

PAINT FOR FABRIC: PLAID FOLKART ACRYLICS
DG = DELTA GLEAMS

AP = PLAID FOLKART ARTIST'S PIGMENTS

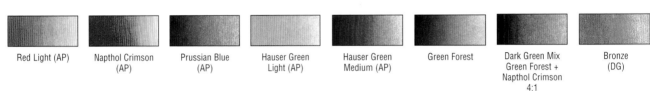

| Red Light (AP) | Napthol Crimson (AP) | Prussian Blue (AP) | Hauser Green Light (AP) | Hauser Green Medium (AP) | Green Forest | Dark Green Mix Green Forest + Napthol Crimson 4:1 | Bronze (DG) |

These patterns may be hand-traced or photocopied for personal use only. Enlarge at 145% to bring them up to full size.

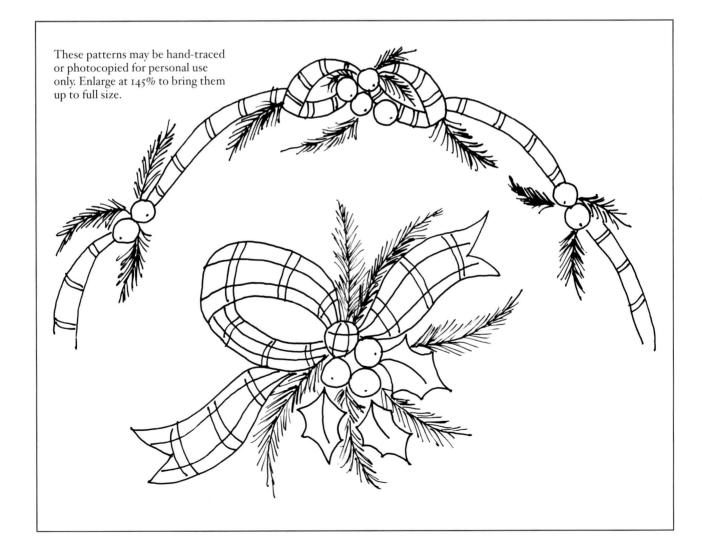

Plaid Ribbon

1

Use lint-free paper towels and rubbing alcohol to clean the surface. Apply the pattern to the rim of the plate using tracing paper and wax-free transfer paper. With a no. 2 shader, basecoat the ribbon with Red using the ribbon stroke (see page 16).

2

Once the basecoated ribbon has thoroughly dried, use your 5/0 liner to outline the ribbon with Green. Notice that where the ribbon turns, the Green crosses over the top of the Red.

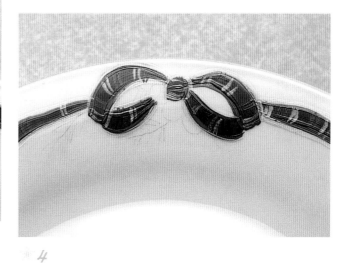

3

Once the Green has thoroughly dried, use your 5/0 liner to outline the Green with Gold all the way around. This won't be real obvious; the Gold is very translucent and it will just add some sparkle to the ribbon. Don't worry if the Gold line gets fatter and thinner; just try to hold the brush up on the tip as much as possible.

4

Still using the 5/0 liner, paint the plaid lines that go across the ribbon, first using Green, then Gold.

Pine Needles and Blueberries

5

Make a dark green mixture using equal parts of Green and Blue 1:1, then add a tiny amount of Red (just enough to darken it a bit more). Use the 5/o liner to stroke in the dark pine needles. Lighten the mixture with White and add the lighter value pine needles.

6

Paint the blueberries with a dark blue mixture of Red, Green, and Blue 1:1:3. Double load your 5/o liner with the dark blue mixture and White and add some final highlights to the berries.

7

Bake the plate following the paint manufacturer's instructions.

Napkin and Table Runner

Painting on fabric is fun and easy. Shading and highlighting can be added to the painted area immediately because the fabric keeps the paints workable long enough for other colors to be softly blended in.

There are two popular techniques for painting on fabric when using fabric medium and acrylic paints. Use the one that's most comfortable for you.

The first technique is to mix 2 parts acrylic paint with 1 part fabric medium and apply to the fabric. Shade and highlight while the area is still damp. Fabric medium does not need to be added to the shading and highlighting colors if they are applied directly over other colors that do contain the fabric medium.

The second technique is to apply fabric medium first to the fabric. Keep the medium slightly inside the pattern lines so that when you apply the paint it will not run outside the design. Scrub the selected colors directly into the fabric that you have covered with medium, then add shading and highlights.

Practice each technique on some scrap fabric to see which one you prefer, then follow steps 8 through 14 to paint the napkin and table runner.

Remember, the acrylic paints used for fabric are different from the acrylic enamels used for china and glass. See the color chart on page 78 for the paint brands and colors I used for the table runner and napkin.

8

Transfer the pattern onto the fabric using transfer paper and tracing paper. Lay deli paper, freezer paper or a paper palette under the cloth while painting to protect the surface you are working on. Use your no. 4 filbert and scrub Napthol Crimson into the center area of the ribbon.

9

Mix a touch of White into Red Light to make a lighter red, and with the no. 4 filbert, highlight the ribbon randomly. Finish painting and highlighting all the Red areas before going on to the Green areas.

Still using the same brush and Hauser Green Medium, paint the green stripes on either side of the red stripe. Highlight the outside edges of the green with a little White, blending the colors together. Complete all of the Green areas before going on.

10

Place a dab of Delta Gleams Bronze on your palette and mix in enough fabric medium to allow it to flow freely. Then load your 5/0 liner with the thinned Bronze and outline the ribbon on both sides of each color as shown.

Holly Leaves and Pine Needles

11

Darken Green Forest with just a touch of Napthol Crimson and with your no. 4 filbert, apply this along the center and bottom of each holly leaf.

12

Still using the same brush, fill in the rest of the leaf area with Hauser Green Light, then blend together. Touch in a tiny bit of White along the leaf centers and along the top edges.

13

Add Green Forest to Napthol Crimson 4:1 and use your 5/0 liner to outline the shaded side of the leaves. Use the same dark green mixture with fabric medium to add pine branches. Be sure to use plenty of the fabric medium on your brush to help force the paint into the fabric. Use Hauser Green Light with fabric medium and add a few lighter green needles on the branches.

Staying within the Bronze outline on the ribbon, add the final green stripes going across, using the dark green mixture and your 5/0 liner. Next to the dark stripes add two stripes using the Gleams Bronze. Finally, add the two dark green stripes on each side of the red center stripe to complete the plaid ribbon.

Berries

14

Mix Prussian Blue with fabric medium on your palette and load a no. 2 filbert. Basecoat the blueberries. Double load the same brush with Prussian Blue and White and stroke in little highlights on the bottom half of each berry.

Apply the little red holly berries with the large ball end of your stylus using Napthol Crimson and fabric medium. Just push them on in groups of three. If you want larger berries, just spread them out a little with your stylus.

For added permanency on the fabric pieces, after the paint is completely dry, press the fabric on the wrong side with a hot iron to heat-set the colors into the fabric.

The table runner at right was painted with a plaid ribbon design similar to the one painted on the white china plate. Along with the napkin, they make a cheerful ensemble for a holiday table.

Christmas Roses

G IVE YOURSELF A GIFT — TAKE A LITTLE TIME EACH DAY TO PRACTICE PAINTING THIS SIMPLE ROSE BY FOLLOWING THESE STEP-BY-STEP INSTRUCTIONS UNTIL YOU HAVE IT MASTERED. YOU'LL BE SURPRISED AT HOW EASY THIS ROSE IS TO PAINT.

ROSES ARE ALWAYS ELEGANT, EVEN AT CHRISTMAS, AND A SET OF HANDPAINTED TABLEWARE IS A TRULY ELEGANT GIFT. I AM GIVING A SET TO MY OLDEST SISTER, SHIRLEY, WHOM I LOVE AND ADORE, AS A SWEET THANK-YOU FOR BEING A WONDERFUL "BIG SIS."

ROYAL BRUSHES

Series SG4010 Soft-Grip White Nylon no. 2 short shader;
Series SG4000 Soft-Grip White Nylon no. 2 round.

ADDITIONAL SUPPLIES

Rubbing alcohol, lint-free paper towels, tracing paper, Scotch tape.

SURFACE

Clear glass goblet from any craft or home supply store.

Pattern and Paints

PAINT: LIQUITEX GLOSSIES

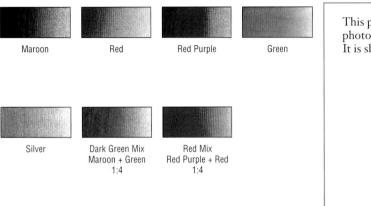

Maroon

Red

Red Purple

Green

Silver

Dark Green Mix
Maroon + Green
1:4

Red Mix
Red Purple + Red
1:4

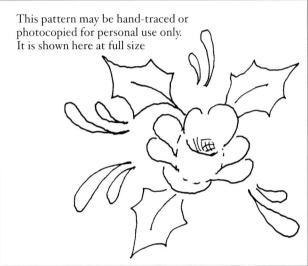

This pattern may be hand-traced or photocopied for personal use only. It is shown here at full size

Rose Petals

1

Clean the surface using lint-free paper towels and rubbing alcohol. Make as many copies of the pattern as you need and randomly tape the roses inside the glass as shown, wherever you like.

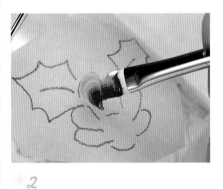

2

Mix Red Purple and Red 1:4 and double load your no. 2 shader with this red mixture and White. (Use this same paint mixture through step 8.) Keeping the White facing upward, begin the Rose on the chisel edge of your brush. Press down while pivoting to create a C-shaped stroke.

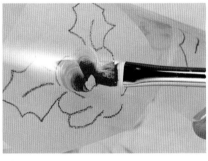

3

Paint a second C-shaped stroke next to the first; this almost forms a heart shape.

Rose Petals

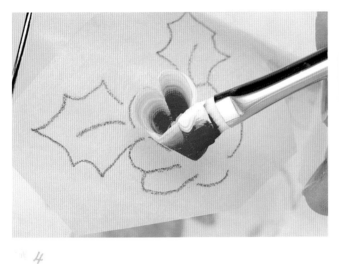

4

The next stroke is a very important stroke—it forms the front petal of the rose. Begin on the chisel edge of the brush and slide down on the left side. Press down on the bristles, and then slide across.

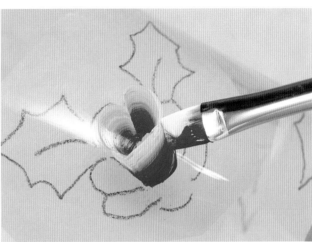

5

Lift back up to the chisel edge as you slide up on the right to finish the stroke.

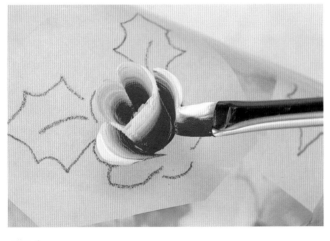

6

Continuing with the same paint mixture and your no. 2 shader, add the first two side-petals. These petals are simple comma strokes (see page 15). Press down at the top of the stroke, then lift to a point.

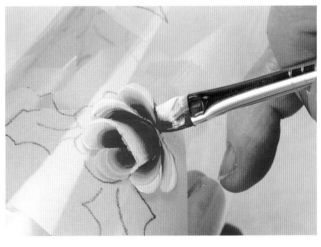

7

Turn your surface to make stroking easier. Add the next two side-petals below the last two in the same manner. These should be close but not touching and right below the previous side-petals.

Rose Petals and Leaves

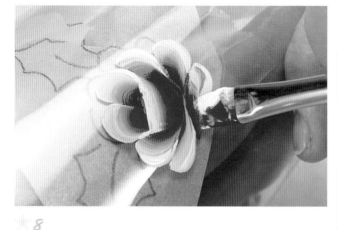

#8

Paint the little petal at the very bottom. This petal is created using a chisel edge comma stroke. Keep the brush next to the bottom of the rose. Begin on the chisel edge then press and slide up to the chisel. You may start your stroke on either the left or right side of the petal, whichever is easier for you.

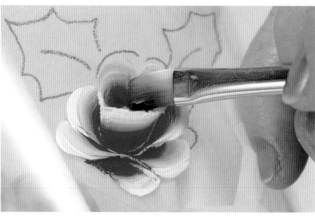

#9

Dab in the bowl (inside) of the rose. Sideload the same brush with Maroon and, while holding the brush vertically, make little dabbing touches into the center.

#10

Add a small float of Maroon for depth and shading at the outside bottom of the bowl as shown.

Use the same no. 2 shader brush to paint the rose and the leaves.

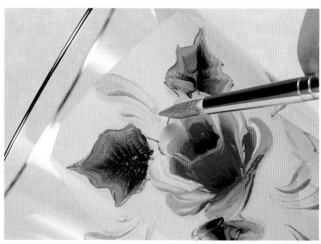

#11

Double load the dark green mix (Maroon and Green 1:4) with White on your no. 2 shader and add the leaves using shape-following strokes (see page 13). Keep the White facing out on all of the leaf edges.

With your no. 2 round and Silver, add the silver comma strokes around the roses and leaves. Make a longer comma, then tuck a shorter one underneath.

Red Glassware and Ornaments

12
Use the end of your brush to add dip-dots in groups of three throughout. Or use a dulled toothpick for smaller dip-dots. Bake the glass according to the paint manufacturer's instructions.

1 The red glass items are painted using the same techniques but with the following color changes:
• The roses are the same colors.
• The leaves are Pine Green and White.
• The comma strokes and dip-dots are Metallic Gold instead of Silver.

2 The ball ornaments are painted the same as the clear glass goblet. The ornaments were then trimmed with glitter (see project 15 for instructions) using Gloss Medium & Varnish stroked on, then sprinkled with Gold or Green Glitter. Some of the leaves were outlined with the varnish and then sprinkled with glitter to make a sparkling outline.

3 The stems of the leaves on the clear glass plate (above left) are painted with the same dark green mixture used on the goblet: Maroon and Green 1:4.

Angel Flowerpot

I ALWAYS PAINTED ANGELS FOR MY WONDERFUL MOTHER-IN-LAW. I HAVE NAMED THIS ANGEL RUBYE IN HER MEMORY AND I WILL ALWAYS REMEMBER WHAT A SWEET ANGEL SHE WAS.

THIS PROJECT IS PAINTED ON A MATTE FINISH FLOWERPOT WHICH CAN BE FOUND AT MANY CRAFT AND DISCOUNT STORES. SINCE THE SURFACE IS NOT HIGHLY GLAZED, YOU CAN USE REGULAR BOTTLED ACRYLIC PAINT.

BE CREATIVE WITH THIS LITTLE ANGEL DESIGN. TRY MAKING THE ANGEL LARGER OR SMALLER, OR ADDING OR ELIMINATING THE HEART-SHAPED LIGHTS. IF YOU WOULD LIKE TO ADD A SECOND ANGEL FACING THE FIRST, JUST FLIP THE PATTERN. USE YOUR IMAGINATION AND MOST OF ALL, HAVE FUN!

ROYAL BRUSHES

Series SG595 Soft-Grip Gold Taklon 5/0 short liner; Series SG4000 Soft-Grip White Nylon no. 2 round; Series 589 White Taklon 5/0 script liner; Series 2700 Royal Aqualon 1/2-inch (12mm) flat; Series 2150 Royal Aqualon no. 10 flat; Series 5005 Sable no. 14.

ADDITIONAL SUPPLIES

Large household brush, foam brush, round artist's sponge, black gesso, white transfer paper, tracing paper, stylus, semi-gloss acrylic varnish.

SURFACE

Unglazed flower pot from any craft, hobby or home supply store.

Pattern and Paints

PAINT: PLAID FOLKART   **AP = PLAID FOLKART ARTIST'S PIGMENTS**   **DG = DELTA GLEAMS**

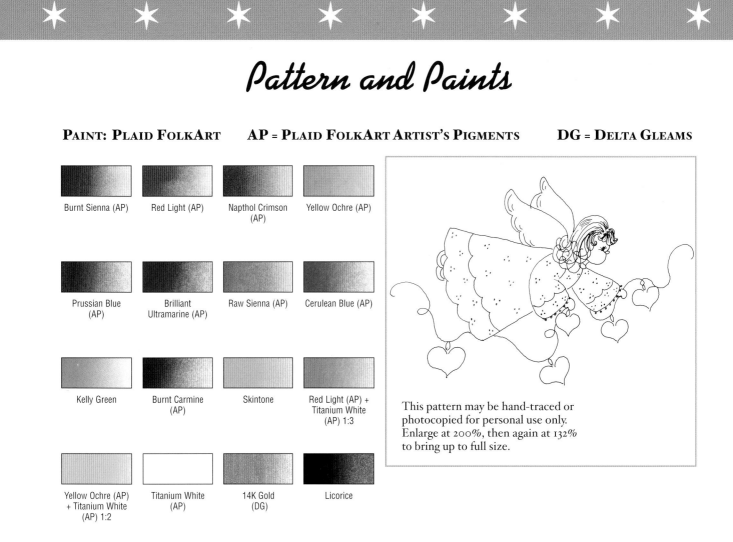

Burnt Sienna (AP)

Red Light (AP)

Napthol Crimson (AP)

Yellow Ochre (AP)

Prussian Blue (AP)

Brilliant Ultramarine (AP)

Raw Sienna (AP)

Cerulean Blue (AP)

Kelly Green

Burnt Carmine (AP)

Skintone

Red Light (AP) + Titanium White (AP) 1:3

Yellow Ochre (AP) + Titanium White (AP) 1:2

Titanium White (AP)

14K Gold (DG)

Licorice

This pattern may be hand-traced or photocopied for personal use only. Enlarge at 200%, then again at 132% to bring up to full size.

Use a foam brush to basecoat the pot inside and out with black gesso. When the gesso has dried use a large house-hold paint brush to undercoat the pot with Prussian Blue. Use a round artist's sponge to sponge on Prussian Blue, Brilliant Ultramarine and Titanium White. Just dip the sponge into one color, then dab the sponge onto the palette to blend the paint on the sponge slightly. Don't mix these colors together; dab one color at a time onto the pot without washing the sponge between colors. Allow to thoroughly dry before proceeding.

Use tracing paper with white transfer paper to trace the pattern onto the surface. With a ¹/₂-inch (12mm) flat, basecoat the dress with Napthol Crimson, the wings with Ivory White, the hair with Yellow Ochre. For the face use Skintone or the flesh tone of your choice. It will take two coats of each color to cover well. Allow to dry between coats.

Shading and Painting the Face

3

Use your ½-inch (12mm) flat to float Burnt Carmine for shading into all the areas as shown. Pull some color from her waist into the skirt for folds in the fabric.

4

Using the same brush, float a highlight of Red Light on the arms and around the dress. This will be very subtle.

5

Use your no. 14 sable with Red Light to tap in the rosy color to the cheek. Mix a lighter highlight color of Red Light and White 1:3 and float a highlight onto her dress—these are just touches accenting the previous highlight.

6

Float Burnt Sienna onto the hands and around the hairline using your no. 10 flat. Also shade the area where the eye will be placed.

7

Use your 5/0 liner and Licorice to add the eye—it is shaped like a teardrop without the pointy top. Also add a few eyelashes. Use the same brush and Titanium White to add a highlight to the upper right corner.

Use Raw Sienna and your 5/0 liner to swirl the hair. If you get swirls you don't like, then just go back in with Yellow Ochre and correct them.

When placing the high-light in the eye, it may help to imagine a clock face, then place the highlight at two o'clock.

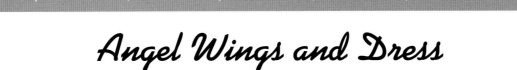

Angel Wings and Dress

8

Now add a few Burnt Sienna swirls to the hair, just a few. Mix Yellow Ochre and Titanium White 1:2 to make a very light highlight. Add a few highlights here and there to brighten the hair up some; make these strokes light and loose, and don't try to add too many.

9

Using your ½-inch (12mm) flat, float 14K Gold onto the back wing and down the back and lower section of the front wing. Float a few C-shaped strokes onto the wings to add some texture. Use your 5/0 liner and 14K Gold to add just a couple of golden highlights in her hair.

10

Load your no. 2 liner with 14K Gold and add some comma strokes to the band on the dress; also reinforce the tips of the wings with some comma strokes. Use your 5/0 liner and Licorice (thinned slightly) to add the little lines and dots on each side of the band; also add the shoes.

11

Use the small end of the stylus and 14K Gold to add the gold dip-dots in sets of three. Also add tiny Titanium White dots along the edge of the sleeve, around the neckline and on the bottom of the dress, to look like lace.

Heart Lights

12

With your no. 2 flat, basecoat the heart-shaped lights with Cerulean Blue, Kelly Green, Red Light and Yellow Ochre; allow to dry. To highlight each heart, use the same brush double loaded with the basecoat color and Titanium White. Keep the white toward the outside edges.

Add the loops and the string using 14k Gold on a 5/0 script liner. Use Titanium White and the same brush to add the little dot-and-comma highlights on each heart.

13

When dry, varnish with three coats of your favorite varnish. I prefer a semi-gloss acrylic varnish.

This design can be used on many surfaces. Be sure to use the correct paint for the surface that you choose.

Etched Projects

Etching is an easy way to add sophisticated elegance to your holiday table. It's also great for accenting painted glass pieces with etched borders. The Etched designs on these wine glasses and mirror coasters were done with simple stencils and an etching product called Etchall.

Etchall is non-toxic and reusable; after etching just pour the Etchall back into its container and use it for another project.

The Poinsettia Stencil and the Holly-and-Berries Stencil I designed for this project are available from the Etchall Company (see resources, page 125). Or make your own stencils from the patterns on the next page.

MATERIALS

Rubbing alcohol, lint-free paper towels, Etchall Creme, Etchall Dip 'n Etch, Etchall applicator bottle with tips, stencils, brayer (included with my stencils), contact paper, water, plastic 2-liter bottle, scissors or craft knife, permanent marking pen, rubber gloves.

SURFACES

Small mirrored coasters and wine glasses
from any craft, discount or home supply store.

Patterns

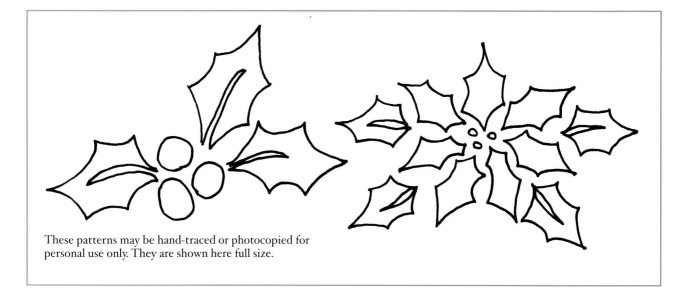

These patterns may be hand-traced or photocopied for personal use only. They are shown here full size.

Applying the Stencil

1

Clean the surface with rubbing alcohol and lint-free paper towels. Use stencils with a sticky backing. Lay the corner of the stencil down so that it is even with the corner of the mirror. Begin to pull off the backing and use your little brayer tool to follow and smooth out any bubbles as you continue to remove the backing.

2

Separate the stencil from the protective cover; pull the cover back while using the brayer to make sure the stencil is smooth.

Etching the Mirror

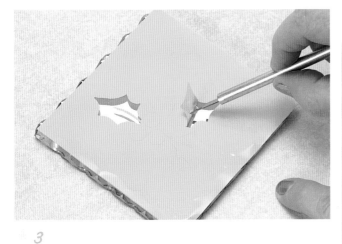

3

Use a craft knife to lift the holly leaf and berry shapes out of the center of the stencil. Use the brayer to smooth the stencil again; make sure the edges around the cut-out areas are smooth and tight to the surface.

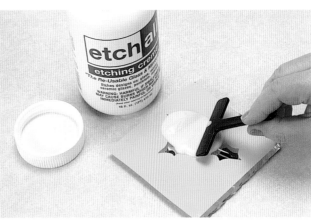

4

Pour a little Etchall Creme onto the surface and spread with the brayer. (Wear rubber gloves if your skin is sensitive.) Allow the cream to sit for 15 minutes.

5

Take the mirror to your sink, turn on the water and let it run for a few seconds to wet the sink (running water protects the sink from the glass etching material and neutralizes it). Rinse off the Etchall Creme under running water. Remove the stencil. After the surface is dry, add freehand curlicues to the design using the Etchall Creme in a small-tipped plastic applicator bottle. Allow the cream to sit for 15 minutes, then rinse it off under running water. Let dry.

You can also use contact paper and cut your own stencils if you like.

Etching the Wine Glass Stem

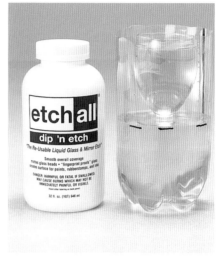

1

Use scissors or a craft knife to cut the top off of a clean 2-liter plastic bottle. You will be etching the stem of the wine glass first. Fill the glass with water (this adds weight to the glass so it will remain steady) and set it inside the 2-liter bottle. Be sure the surface that the 2-liter bottle is sitting on is level; also be sure the wine glass is sitting level inside of the 2-liter bottle. Fill the 2-liter with water up to the exact line where you want the stem to be etched.

2

Remove the glass from the 2-liter. With a fine-point marking pen, mark the side of the 2-liter exactly where the height of the water is with the glass removed.

3

Pour the water out of the 2-liter and dry the inside with a paper towel (don't pour the water out of the wine glass). Pour Etchall Dip 'n Etch into the 2-liter up to the line that you marked. (Wear rubber gloves if you have sensitive skin.)

Now set the glass (still filled with water) into the Dip 'n Etch. Allow it to sit for 15 minutes; don't take it out before the time is up.

Etchall's etching creams and fluids are non-toxic, but they may burn if you have sensitive skin. I have never had any problems with them, but you may want to take the precaution of wearing rubber gloves.

4

Remove the wine glass from the Dip 'n Etch and rinse it under running water. Let dry. Carefully pour the remainder of the Dip 'n Etch back into its original container for reuse.

Etching the Holly Leaf Design

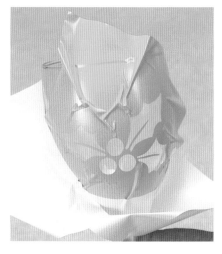

5

Clean the top section of the glass with lint-free paper towels and rubbing alcohol. Apply the stencil to the outside of the glass as you did on the mirror. Since it's on a rounded form, however, it won't be real smooth around the edges; this is okay. The most important part of the stencil to have smoothed is the area immediately around the pattern openings where you will be applying the Etchall Creme. Look inside of the glass and you'll be able to see if the pattern edges are properly adhered.

Cut a small rectangle of contact paper and use this to form a little apron underneath the stencil. This will catch any drippings that might slide off (which usually doesn't happen). Apply the Etchall Creme and let it sit for 15 minutes. Then use the brayer to remove the Etchall Creme and place it back into the original container for reuse.

6

Rinse the glass under running water to remove the etching cream. Then remove the stencil to expose the beautiful etched design. Let dry.

Folk Art Christmas

I T'S HARD TO BELIEVE THIS TRADITIONALLY PAINTED CANDLE HOLDER START-ED OUT AS A PLAIN OLD PICKLE JAR! I USED ETCHALL'S DIP 'N ETCH TO GIVE THE JAR ITS FROSTED ELEGANCE. THE ETCHING PROCESS PROVIDES A PER-FECT SURFACE THAT WILL ACCEPT REGULAR ACRYLIC PAINTS. PROJECT 12 SHOWS YOU HOW TO EASILY ETCH ANY GLASS SURFACE.

USE THIS JAR TO HOLD GOODIES OR ADD A CANDLE TO LIGHT UP YOUR CHRISTMAS. I USED TRADITIONAL CHRISTMAS COLORS ALONG WITH BRIGHT BLUE AND SOFT YEL-LOW TO MAKE A PRETTY FOLK ART DESIGN THAT CAN BE USED ALL YEAR LONG.

ROYAL BRUSHES

Series SG595 Soft-Grip Gold Taklon 5/0 short liner; Series 2250 Royal Aqualon no. 4 round; Series 2150 Royal Aqualon no. 6 flat; Series 2150 Royal Aqualon no. 2 flat.

ADDITIONAL SUPPLIES

Transfer paper, tracing paper, etching supplies, ribbons.

SURFACE

Clear glass jar. The ornaments are metal cutouts found in craft and home supply stores.

Paint and Patterns

PAINT: PLAID FOLKART   AP = PLAID FOLKART ARTIST'S PIGMENTS

Lipstick Red	Cerulean Blue (AP)	Turner's Yellow (AP)	Thicket	Titanium White (AP)	Raw Sienna (AP)

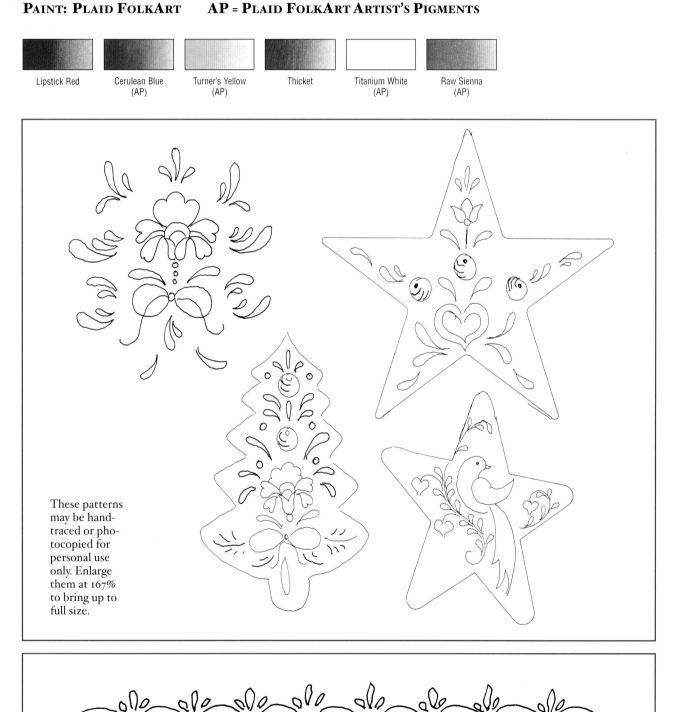

These patterns may be hand-traced or photocopied for personal use only. Enlarge them at 167% to bring up to full size.

This pattern is for the border design around the top of the jar. It may be hand-traced or photocopied for personal use only. It is shown here full size.

Flower and Ribbon

✳ *1*

Use any type of clean, clear glass jar such as the pickle jar shown here, and follow the etching directions in project 12, page 100 to etch the outside of the jar. After rinsing off the etching cream, let the jar dry completely before painting on it.

✳ *2*

Apply the pattern to your etched jar using tracing paper and transfer paper. Fill in the top of the center flower using Turner's Yellow and your no. 6 flat. You will need two coats; allow to thoroughly dry between coats. Double load Cerulean Blue and Titanium White on your no. 2 flat, stroke this across the bottom of the flower. Using the same colors and brush, add the bow using the ribbon stroke (see page 16); keep the white toward the outside.

✳ *3*

Double load Raw Sienna and Turner's Yellow onto the no. 6 flat and shade the bottom of the yellow flower, keep the Raw Sienna next to the blue. Highlight the top of the flower by double loading Titanium White and Turner's Yellow; make three little C-shaped strokes. Using your no. 6 flat, float Raw Sienna on the bottom of the flower, then highlight with your 5/o liner and Titanium White.

Comma Strokes and Rosebud

4

The strokes in this step are all comma strokes using the no. 4 round. The side petal strokes are Lipstick Red, and the over-strokes are a lighter value mixture of Lipstick Red and Titanium White 1:1. Use the same brush but apply less pressure for the over-strokes; using less pressure makes the stroke smaller. Load the brush with Thicket and fill in the calyx of the flower with just two comma strokes; fill in the dot at the bottom of the calyx with the 5/0 liner and Thicket. Use your 5/0 liner and Titanium White to add the little white lines on the top part of the flower.

5

Load your no. 4 round with Thicket then tip the point in Titanium White; add the green comma strokes as shown. Reload your brush after each stroke so each comma shape stays nice and round. Sometimes the White will show more in some strokes than in others; that's fine. It gives your work that handpainted look.

6

On either side of the jar I painted little rosebud designs just like the ones on the large metal star ornament shown at right on the next page. Base in this rose using a no. 2 flat and Lipstick Red. Shade along the bottom with a double load of Lipstick Red and Cerulean Blue (the Cerulean Blue will darken the red).

7

Mix Lipstick Red and Titanium White 1:1 to make a pink and use your 5/0 liner to add three little comma strokes in the circle. Add the little center dot with Turner's Yellow.

#8

With your no. 4 round, add the blue comma strokes using Cerulean Blue tipped in Titanium White. Use the handle end of your liner brush to add the dip-dots; the single dots are Turner's Yellow, the sets of three dots are Lipstick Red. Repeat some of these comma strokes and dip-dots where the rosebuds are on the sides of the jar.

With the no. 4 round, add the final border strokes all around the top and bottom of the jar. Use Lipstick Red for the comma strokes; these are painted end to end and almost touching. Use Thicket to add the three little green finishing strokes between the commas, and Turner's Yellow for the little yellow dots around the top.

Let the paint dry completely, then embellish the jar with a ribbon and bow in a coordinating color.

These folk art designs look great on antiqued metal ornaments cut into holiday shapes. They're created using the same strokes you used for the etched jar; you will also use the same colors for each specific motif. See page 104 for the ornament patterns.

The blue bird is basecoated with equal parts of Cerulean Blue and White. Shade the dark area with Cerulean Blue using the floated color technique. Float White on the breast of the bird and top of the tail.

The body and tail of the yellow bird are basecoated with Turner's Yellow, shaded with Raw Sienna and highlighted with White. Use floated color for shading and highlighting. The wing is basecoated with Bright Red and the top of the wing is highlighted with White.

Winter Landscape

I WAS INTRODUCED TO ART BY LEARNING TO PAINT SCENERY ON CANVAS WITH OIL PAINTS. I STILL LOVE PAINTING LITTLE LANDSCAPE SCENES AND ACRYLIC PAINTS HAVE MADE THIS EVEN MORE ENJOYABLE. YOU'LL FIND THESE DESIGNS QUICK AND FUN TO PAINT, AND BECAUSE THEY ARE SO SMALL, THEY DON'T REQUIRE A LOT OF DETAIL.

THE ROUND AND STAR-SHAPED PORCELAIN ORNAMENTS HAVE A MATTE SURFACE AND CAN BE PAINTED WITH REGULAR ACRYLIC PAINTS. BEFORE PAINTING THE SCENE ON THE GLASS HURRICANE LAMP, I ETCHED THE AREA TO GIVE IT SOME TOOTH; PROJECT 12 SHOWS YOU HOW TO DO THIS.

★

ROYAL BRUSHES

Series SG595 Soft-Grip 5/0 liner; Series 2150 Royal Aqualon no. 2 and no. 6 flats; Series 2170 Royal Aqualon no. 4 filbert; Series 5005 Langnickel no. 8 sable.

★

ADDITIONAL SUPPLIES

Old toothbrush, tracing paper, transfer paper, ballpoint pen or stylus.

★

SURFACE

Porcelain ornaments by Provo Craft and glass hurricane lamp can be found at craft, hobby or home supply stores.

Paint and Patterns

PAINT: PLAID FOLKART ACRYLIC **AP = PLAID FOLKART ARTIST'S PIGMENTS**

M = PLAID FOLKART METALLICS **DC = DELTA CERAMCOAT ACRYLIC**

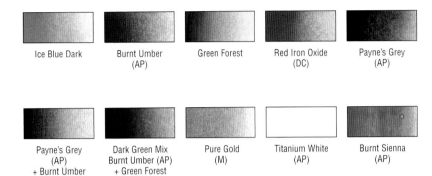

Ice Blue Dark | Burnt Umber (AP) | Green Forest | Red Iron Oxide (DC) | Payne's Grey (AP)

Payne's Grey (AP) + Burnt Umber (AP) (1:1) | Dark Green Mix Burnt Umber (AP) + Green Forest (1:1) | Pure Gold (M) | Titanium White (AP) | Burnt Sienna (AP)

These patterns may be hand-traced or photocopied for personal use only. They are shown here full size.

Snow-covered Hills and Red Barn

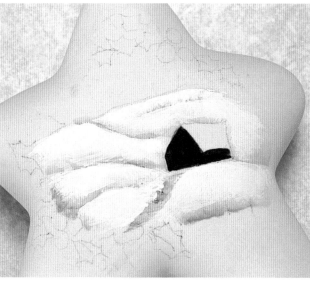

Use transfer paper and tracing paper to trace the pattern onto the ornament. Lightly float Burnt Sienna on your no. 6 flat to separate the background hills from the foreground. This is very light and transparent. Also corner load the brush with Burnt Sienna and paint the dirt road by jiggling the flat of the brush as you move it forward.

Basecoat the front and side of the barn with Red Iron Oxide on a no. 2 flat. Let dry. Use your no. 14 sable and Titanium White to tap in the snow onto the tops of the hills. Don't overwork the paint.

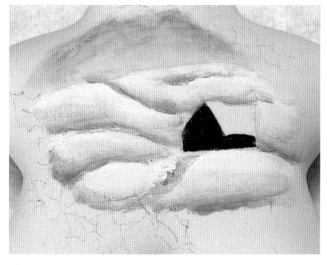

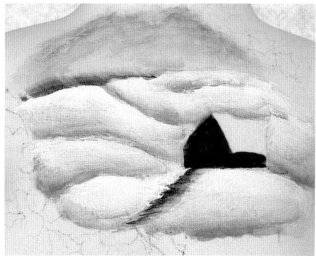

To shade the snow, sideload a no. 6 flat with Ice Blue Dark. Float this right over the Burnt Sienna and walk the color (see page 14) up into the hills.

　To paint the sky, just flip the same brush so the color is at the top and add the sky by walking the brush down to the hills.

Still using your no. 6 flat, float a dark shadow of Burnt Umber right behind the topmost hill. While you have this color in your brush, darken the road from the barn door forward. Keep the brush horizontal and use tiny back and forth strokes to give it a rustic, uneven look.

Barn and Background Trees

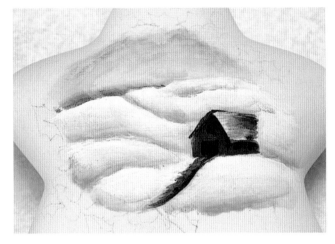

With the no. 6 flat, use a float of Payne's Grey to shade the barn under the eaves and under the roof on the side. Mix Burnt Umber and Payne's Grey 1:1 and just touch some color onto the roof. The roof will later have snow on it. With Payne's Grey on a 5/0 liner, add the door and windows. Add a touch of Burnt Umber to your brush and darken the right side of the road.

Double load a tiny bit of Green Forest and Titanium White on the very tip of your no. 8 sable and just lightly touch in two rows of evergreen trees in the background hills.

Take a tiny bit of Red Iron Oxide and Titanium White on the corner of your no. 2 flat and pull in a suggestion of boards on the front of the barn. Use a 5/0 liner with Burnt Umber and Payne's Grey 1:1 to pull up little stick trees around and on top of all the evergreens. Also add a few of the stick trees to the background hills (don't get carried away, just add a few).

Pull some little squiggles up from the path to look like dead grass. Add the fence posts and cross boards now; these will look different when finished since they will be covered with snow.

Snow and Foreground Trees

8

Now add the covering of snow. Load a lot of Titanium White on your no. 4 filbert and dab snow onto the back edge of the barn roof. Just tap this on; the paint will be rather thick.

9

Tap more snow onto the front of the barn and then slide a little over onto the dark part of the roof. Also tap some snow onto the hilltops, fence and the road. Dab in some clouds in the sky; soften them with your little finger if they are too obvious.

10

There are two large pine trees next to the barn. The back tree (the one on the right) is painted with Burnt Umber and Green Forest 1:1 on a no. 2 flat. Paint the trees by starting with one vertical tap for the top of the tree then use light back-and-forth horizontal taps for the body of the tree (see page 15). Tap a little Titanium White on the right edge of the back tree. To paint the pine tree in front, use a double loaded brush of Green Forest and Titanium White.

Reapply the pattern and trace on the large bare tree on the left side. Use your 5/0 liner with Burnt Umber to paint the tree.

Holly Leaves and Final Touches

11

The first side of each holly leaf is painted with Green Forest on a no. 2 flat. The second side of each leaf is painted with a double load of Green Forest and Titanium White. Keep the white facing out while you stroke in the leaves. Float a very light float of Red Iron Oxide onto the dark sides of some of the leaves. This last float will not be real noticeable but it is important because it adds harmony in the overall design. Do not float every leaf, but just a random selection. Paint the berries using your 5/0 liner and Red Iron Oxide. Use Red Iron Oxide with a touch of Titanium White to highlight half of each berry.

With the same brush and thinned Burnt Umber, add curlicues. You can also use Pure Gold to add comma strokes if you like. To finish, use an old toothbrush with Titanium White and spatter some snowflakes onto the ornament.

If you want to paint this pretty country scene on a glass surface such as the hurricane lamp, first etch the glass with an area large enough for the entire design to fit nicely. (Refer to the etching techniques demonstrated in Project 12.) The etching creates a tooth that can be painted on with regular acrylic paints. The etching also makes a much softer effect when a candle is lit from the inside.

The round porcelain ornament is painted using all the same colors and techniques described in this project for the star-shaped ornament. The only additional color is the house in the foreground, which is painted with Turner's Yellow and shaded with Burnt Sienna.

Glitter Ornaments

THE WONDERFUL GLITTER ORNAMENTS WE ARE FINDING NOW AT CHRISTMASTIME ARE AN ECHO OF THE PAST. I'M SO GLAD THEIR POPULARITY HAS BEEN REVIVED AS THEY BRING BACK SUCH WARM MEMORIES FOR ME. I REMEMBER HOW CAREFULLY WE PLACED THE BEAUTIFUL GLITTERED TREASURES IN SPECIAL PROMINENCE ON OUR TREE. NOWADAYS I ESPECIALLY LIKE THE POLYFLAKE IRIDESCENT GLITTER I USED IN THIS PROJECT; IT IS ULTRAFINE AND DOESN'T FALL OFF THE ORNAMENT LIKE THE LARGER GLITTER CAN. ITS SPARKLE AND SHINE IS UNMATCHED WHEN HIGHLIGHTED BY THE GLOWING LIGHTS OF THE TREE.

ROYAL BRUSH

Series SG595 Soft-Grip no. 2 short liner (or your favorite
brush that allows you to create beautiful strokes).

ADDITIONAL SUPPLIES

Liquitex Gloss Medium & Varnish; Leafing Adhesive Pen (made by
ColArt and used for gold leafing); lid of a box or a large paper plate (to catch
the loose glitter); PolyFlake iridescent glitter made by the Glitterex Corp., available at
craft stores; loose glitter in different colors of your choice;
a soft makeup brush to brush off excess glitter.

SURFACE

Glass ornaments in your choice of colors
from any craft or discount store.

Supplies for Glitter Ornaments

After extensive experimentation with many different products, I have come to the conclusion that the specific products I have listed in these instructions are the best for this glitter ornament project. For example, the Liquitex Gloss Medium & Varnish. This no ordinary varnish. It has the same binder that is mixed with dry pigment to make paint and it is superior to the strongest glue. It is a flexible medium so it does not crack, which makes it ideal for this application. Because it has the same consistency as acrylic paint, it can be stroked on and will hold its shape exactly as if you were using acrylic paint. That's why I think it is so perfect for making these glitter ornaments. You simply stroke on the design using your paintbrush and Liquitex varnish, then sprinkle glitter over the design. The varnish will hold the glitter in place exactly where you stroked it on, creating a beautiful glittered ornament that will last for many years.

If you are not confident about your strokework but love the glittered look, there is a wonderful tool that can help you make beautiful glittered ornaments. This tool is the Leafing Adhesive Pen made by ColArt. Although a pen cannot produce beautiful strokework like a brush can, it will still create pretty designs and personalized script. It is made specifically for writing on glass so the glue will adhere without drawing or puddling and will accept the glitter and hold it permanently. It is so easy to use, you will find yourself glittering everything in sight!

I used both the Liquitex Gloss Medium & Varnish and also the ColArt Leafing Adhesive Pen for the Merry Christmas ornament in this project. You can do the whole project with just one or the other if you like, but I thought it would be fun for you to get acquainted with both products at the same time.

For design ideas, I often refer to vintage Christmas books and old magazines that show old-fashioned ornaments. They gave me the inspiration for several of the beautiful ornaments shown on the facing page.

1

Using your adhesive pen, write Merry Christmas or whatever saying or design you would like on the ornament. When using the adhesive pen, do not set the pen down without placing the cap on it first. It will dry up very quickly and be rendered useless if it is set aside uncapped even for a short time. A general rule to remember is, "If it is not in your hand, it must have the cap on."

2

Pour on the ultrafine loose glitter as soon as the milky white lines from the pen turn clear. Then gently shake off the excess. Make sure you have a box lid under your project to catch the glitter.

3

With the Liquitex Gloss Medium & Varnish and a small brush, make at least four little dots around the top as reference points to help center your design. Below the dots, paint connecting comma strokes around the ornament. Pour the glitter immediately; you do not have as much open time as you did with the adhesive pen.

4

Wait at least an hour for everything to completely dry. Then use a very soft (make-up type) brush to very lightly brush the excess glitter away.

5

It's not necessary to varnish over your glitter, but it is an option if you want to ensure that not another single speck of glitter will ever work its way off the ornament. Just a light touch of varnish over each finished stroke is all that would be needed, but remember, this is optional.

Poured Ornaments

I HAVE A GREAT IDEA— CALL ALL YOUR FAMILY AND FRIENDS TOGETHER AND HAVE A FESTIVE ORNAMENT-MAKING PARTY! THIS IS THE PERFECT TECHNIQUE FOR JUST SUCH A GATHERING. THIS NO-STRESS PROJECT WILL WORK EASILY FOR PEOPLE WHO HAVE NEVER PAINTED BEFORE; AND YOU WILL PRODUCE AN ARRAY OF BEAUTIFUL ORNAMENTS WHILE YOU ARE CREATING WARM AND WONDERFUL MEMORIES. I GUARANTEE SUCCESSFUL ORNAMENTS AND LOTS OF FRIENDLY FUN.

YOU CAN FIND AN ABUNDANCE OF THE CLEAR GLASS ORNAMENTS USED FOR THIS PROJECT IN CRAFT AND DISCOUNT STORES. THEY COME IN ALL SHAPES AND SIZES.

SUPPLIES
Styrofoam cups, paper towels.

SURFACE
Clear glass ornaments from any craft, discount or home supply store.

Paint and Color Information

PAINT: PLAID FOLKART METALLICS

Metallic Rose   Metallic Amethyst   Metallic Blue Sapphire

The three metallic colors shown above are the ones I used for the poured ornament in this project. However, you may choose different ones. They need not be metallic. Using the right colors is the secret to making beautiful poured ornaments. Without going into the intricate details of color theory, I would like to offer a few suggestions that will make your ornaments more vibrant and pleasing to the eye.

When choosing colors, look for bottled acrylics in primary colors that are pure in intensity, not grayed down. These colors will look intense in the bottle, so lay out all of your bottles of paint and pick out the brightest and most intense colors. After the colors are poured into the ornament they will be shaken together which will result in color mixes. Our goal is to pick colors that provide beautiful color combinations when mixed together.

Complementary colors that are very attractive when seen side by side produce lackluster colors when mixed together; so using them next to each other should be avoided when making poured ornaments. They can be used in the same ornament if they are shielded by other colors that mix well with each. For instance, Blue could be used between Red and Green because Blue can be mixed with either Red or Green to make beautiful color combinations. Metallic or Interference Gold is also beautiful to use between two complementary colors, as the colors will be separated from each other and complemented with Gold to create beautiful ornaments.

Here are the complementary color combinations which should *not* be poured side by side in an ornament: Orange and Blue, Red and Green, Yellow and Purple, Purple and Orange, Green and Orange.

Remember that you can use these colors in the same ornament but they should have other colors poured between them so that they do not touch each other. There is an option if you really want to use these colors side by side. Each color must be poured separately and allowed to dry before the next color is poured into the ornament so there is no chance that they will mix together.

If you are in doubt as to which colors will look good together, try mixing two colors on a palette to see how they blend and then you will know if you desire to use them in your ornament.

It's good to have a variety of acrylic paints on hand that include some of the following metallic colors that I have had success with: Gold, Phthalocyanine Blue, Phthalocyanine Green, Viridian or Sap Green, Acra Violet or any combination of Red Violets or Magentas, and Manganese Blue.

Liquitex makes a paint called Interference Paint and it comes in 6 colors. It consists of tiny mica chips suspended in a medium. Interestingly, all six colors appear colorless in the bottle. This can be confusing when you go to buy them. The beauty of each color comes out when combined or laid over other acrylic colors. It produces the most beautiful sheen and has been instrumental to the beauty of many of the poured ornaments I have made.

It is unnecessary to buy all six colors but I believe that having at least two of these colors will ensure success with every ornament that you pour. Interference Gold is the most important color to buy. The next two colors I would suggest purchasing would be Interference Blue and Interference Green. Then if you wish, buy Interference Violet, Red or Orange.

Remember to use metallic, Interference or even glitter paint in your poured ornaments, as these will highly complement your acrylic colors.

Pouring and Shaking

1

Remove the metal hanger from the top of a clear glass ornament. Squirt the first color, Metallic Rose, into the *inside* of the ornament.

2

Immediately pour the second color, Metallic Amethyst. Then pour the third color, Metallic Blue Sapphire.

3

Be sure to leave some clear glass showing here and there.

4

Place a folded paper towel over the hole to protect your finger and shake the ornament until you like the pattern that is showing.

5

Shake out any excess paint into a Styrofoam cup and then set the ornament upside down in the cup for at least 15 minutes to drain.

Final Steps

6

Rotate the ornament a quarter turn every 15 or 20 minutes for several hours. This keeps the colors from all running to one side and keeps the design intact while it is drying. If you are making multiple ornaments, just line them up in their Styrofoam cups and rotate them at the same time.

When dry, replace the hanger and if desired, decorate with ribbons, beads or even glitter.

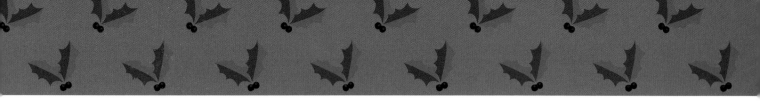

Resources

ColArt
*Liquitex Glossies, Liquitex
Interference Paint,
Leafing Adhesive Pen*
11 Constitution Ave.
Piscataway, NJ 08855
800-445-4278
www.winsornewton.com

Delta Ceramcoat Acrylics
Delta Gleams
Delta Technical Coatings
2550 Pellissier Place
Whittier, CA 91601
800-423-4135
www.deltacrafts.com

Etchall
B&B Products Inc.
18700 N. 107th Avenue, Suite 13
Sun City, AZ 85373
(623) 933-4567
www.etchall.com

Garden Ridge Pottery
19411 Atrium Pl., Suite 170
Houston, TX 77084
www.gardenridge.com

Hobby Lobby
7707 SW 44th Street
Oklahoma City, OK 73179
www.hobbylobby.com

Michaels
800 Bent Branch Dr.
Irving, TX 75063
(972) 409-1300
www.michaels.com

Plaid Enterprises
*FolkArt Acrylics, FolkArt Metallics,
FolkArt Artist's Pigments*
P.O. Box 2835
Norcross, GA 30091-2835
800-842-4197
www.plaidonline.com

Provo Craft
151 E. 3450 North
Spanish Fork, UT 84660
www.provocraft.com

Royal Brush Manufacturing Inc.
*Royal Soft-Grip, Royal Langnickel,
Royal Aqualon brushes*
6707 Broadway
Merrillville, IN 46410
(219) 660-4170
www.royalbrush.com

Retailers in Canada

Crafts Canada
2745 Twenty-ninth St. NE
Calgary, Alberta T1Y 7B5

Folk Art Enterprises
P.O. Box 1088
Ridgetown, Ontario N0P 2C0
(888) 214-0062

MacPherson Craft Wholesale
83 Queen St. E.
P.O. Box 1870
St. Mary's, Ontario N4X 1C2
(519) 284-1741

Maureen McNaughton Enterprises
RR #2
Belwood, Ontario N0B 1J0
(519) 843-5648

Mercury Art & Craft Supershop
332 Wellington St.
London, Ontario N6C 4P7
(519) 434-1636

Town & Country Folk Art Supplies
93 Green Lane
Thornhill, Ontario L3T 6K6
(905) 882-0199

Retailers in United Kingdom

Art Express
Index House
70 Burley Road
Leeds LS3 1JX
Tel: 0800 731 4185
www.artexpress.co.uk

Crafts World (head office only)
No 8 North Street, Guildford
Surrey GU1 4AF
Tel: 07000 757070
Telephone for local store

Chroma Colour Products
Unit 5 Pilton Estate
Pitlake
Croydon CR0 3RA
Tel: 020 8688 1991
www.chromacolour.com

Green & Stone
259 King's Road
London SW3 5EL
Tel: 020 7352 0837
greenandstone@enterprise.net

Hobbycrafts (head office only)
River Court
Southern Sector
Bournemouth International Airport
Christchurch
Dorset BH23 6SE
Tel: 0800 272387 freephone
Telephone for local store

Homecrafts Direct
P.O. Box 38
Leicester LE1 9BU
Tel: 0116 251 3139
Mail order service

Index

Explore your *creative side* with North Light Books

Create classic holiday decorations that everyone will love! You'll find 14 simple painting projects inside, from Santa figures and Christmas card holders to tree ornaments and candy dishes. Each one includes easy-to-follow instructions, step-by-step photographs and simple designs that you can use on candles, fabric or glass.

ISBN 1-58180-237-4, paperback, 112 pages, #32012-K

This book is the must-have one-stop reference for decorative painters, crafters, home decorators and do-it-yourselfers. It's packed with solutions to every painting challenge, including surface preparation, lettering, borders, faux finishes, strokework techniques and more! You'll also find five fun-to-paint projects designed to instruct, challenge and entertain you, no matter what your skill level.

ISBN 1-58180-062-2, paperback, 256 pages, #31803-K

Learn to paint your favorite Christmas themes, including Santas, angels, elves and more, on everything from elegant ornaments to festive photo albums. Renowned decorative painter John Gutcher shows you how with eleven all-new, step-by-step projects. He makes mastering tricky details simple with special tips for painting fur, hair, richly textured clothing and realistic flesh tones.

ISBN 1-58180-105-X, paperback, 128 pages, #31794-K

Fill your home with the timeless charm of folk art scenes! Popular instructors Judy Diephouse and Lynne Deptula team up to show you how to capture the quaint and picturesque beauty of rolling farmland, old-fashioned barns, churches and country gardens. You'll find ten projects for adorning everything from wooden boxes and mitten chests to picnic baskets and lampshades. Easy-to-trace patterns, paint color charts and start-to-finish instructions make each project a joy to create.

ISBN 1-58180-117-3, paperback, 128 pages, #31813-K

These books and other fine North Light titles are available from your local art & craft retailer, bookstore, online supplier or by calling 1-800-448-0915.